Anthropology Career Resources Handbook

prepared by

Margaret A. Gwynne
State University of New York, Stony Brook

Boston   New York   San Francisco
Mexico City   Montreal   Toronto   London   Madrid   Munich   Paris
Hong Kong   Singapore   Tokyo   Cape Town   Sydney

TABLE OF CONTENTS

Graduate Programs
Organizations
Informational Websites

PART THREE: NEXT STEPS

PREFACE

This handbook was prepared for undergraduate anthropology students who are intent on a future career focused on some aspect of applied anthropology: applied cultural anthropology, applied archaeology, applied physical anthropology, or applied anthropological linguistics. In twenty-one chapters, it provides comprehensive lists of

- reading materials (both books and journal articles) pertinent to many different domains of applied anthropology;

- journals relevant to each domain, together with subscription information;

- M.A., Ph.D., and other advanced degree programs to which students may wish to apply in order to prepare for careers in specific domains;

- membership, advocacy, and other domain-relevant organizations students may wish to consider joining or contacting as possible sources of internships or jobs; and

- additional websites where students will find information on each domain of application, as well as links to other relevant sites.

Part One, "Background Studies" (Sections 1-4), contains lists of resources that will help students to develop the conceptual framework they will require in order to become practitioners in any domain of applied anthropology. Part Two, "Domains of Anthropological Practice" (Sections 5-19), lists domain-relevant resources for fifteen career areas in which applied anthropologists work. Part Three, "Next Steps" (Sections 20-21), provides useful information on advanced degree programs and other continuing education opportunities, and on finding a first job as an applied anthropologist.

A student whose career interests are already well-defined should concentrate on Parts One and Three of this book, as well as the single chapter in Part Two containing resource lists relevant to his or her chosen field. For students who have not yet identified a specific domain of applied anthropology on which to focus, a good way to explore various career possibilities is to read one or more of the books and articles listed in the references section for any domain, included in Part Two, that is of potential interest. (Although a few classics are included, most of these references are recently published; older or more peripheral references will be found in the bibliographies of the references listed.) Leafing through the professional journals listed for each domain may also help students to narrow down their fields of potential interest. When possibilities are identified, students can then go on to contact the organizations and explore the informational websites and graduate programs relevant to those domains.

This compendium is neither exhaustive nor flawless. Inevitably, relevant items will have been overlooked, errors will have been introduced, and addresses, telephone numbers, and websites will have changed in the interval between compilation and publication. Users of this handbook who identify oversights or inaccuracies are asked to contact the author at <mgwynne@notes.cc.sunysb.edu>. Additions and corrections will be gratefully received.

PART ONE: BACKGROUND STUDIES

1. DEFINING APPLIED ANTHROPOLOGY

SUGGESTED READINGS

Baba, Marietta L.
1994. "The Fifth Subdiscipline: Anthropological Practice and the Future of Anthropology." Human Organization 53(2):174-186.

2000. "Theories of Practice in Anthropology: A Critical Appraisal." In Hill, Carole E., and Marietta L. Baba (eds.): The Unity of Theory and Practice in Anthropology: Rebuilding a Fractured Synthesis (NAPA Bulletin 18), pp. 17-44. Washington, DC: National Association for the Practice of Anthropology.

Bennett, John
1996. "Applied Anthropology: Ideological and Conceptual Aspects." Current Anthropology 36:S23-S53.

Cerroni-Long, E.L.
1995. Insider Anthropology (NAPA Bulletin No. 17). Washington, DC: National Association for the Practice of Anthropology.

Cleveland, David A.
2000. "Globalization and Anthropology: Expanding the Options." Human Organization 59:370-374.

Dowie, Mark
2001. American Foundations: An Investigative History. Cambridge, MA: MIT Press.

Endicott, Kirk M., and Robert Welsch (eds.)
2001. "Should Cultural Anthropology Model Itself on the Natural Sciences?" In Kirk M. Endicott and Robert Welsch (eds.): Taking Sides: Clashing Views on Contemporary Issues in Anthropology, pp. 178-199. Guilford, CT: McGraw-Hill/Dushkin.

Ervin, Alexander M.
2000. Applied Anthropology: Tools and Perspectives for Contemporary Practice. Boston: Allyn and Bacon.

Fiske, Shirley, J. and Erve Chambers

1995. "The Inventions of Practice." Human Organization 55 (1):1-12.

Gellner, David N.,, and Eric Hirsch (eds.)
2001. Inside Organizations: Anthropologists at Work. Oxford, UK: Berg Publishers.

Higgins, Patricia J., and J. Anthony Paredes
2000. Classics of Practicing Anthropology, 1978-1998. Oklahoma City, OK: Society for Applied Anthropology.

Hill, Carole E.
2000. "Strategic Issues for Rebuilding a Theory and Practice Synthesis." In Hill, Carole E., and Marietta L. Baba (eds.): The Unity of Theory and Practice in Anthropology: Rebuilding a Fractured Synthesis (NAPA Bulletin 18), pp. 1-16. Washington: National Association for the Practice of Anthropology.

Johnsrud, Cris
2000. "Integrating Anthropologists into Non-Academic Work Settings." In Sabloff, Paula L.W. (ed.): Careers in Anthropology: Profiles of Practitioner Anthropologists (NAPA Bulletin no. 20), pp. 95-98. Washington, DC: American Anthropological Association.

Jordan, Ann T.
2000. "Building a Bridge Between Academics and Practice." In Sabloff, Paula L.W. (ed.): Careers in Anthropology: Profiles of Practitioner Anthropologists (NAPA Bulletin no. 20), pp. 85-86. Washington, DC: American Anthropological Association.

Kozaitis, Kathryn A.
2000. "The Rise of Anthropological Praxis." In Hill, Carole E., and Marietta L. Baba (eds.): The Unity of Theory and Practice in Anthropology: Rebuilding a Fractured Synthesis (NAPA Bulletin 18), pp. 45-66. Washington, DC: NAPA.

Kuklick, Henrika
1997. "After Ishmael: The Fieldwork Tradition and its Future." In Gupta, Akhil, and James Ferguson (eds.): Anthropological Locations: Boundaries and Grounds of a Field Science, pp. 47-65. Berkeley: University of California Press.

Kuznar, Lawrence A.
1997. Reclaiming a Scientific Anthropology. Walnut Creek, CA: AltaMira Press.

Lett, James
1997. Science, Reason, and Anthropology: A Guide to Critical Thinking. Blue Ridge Summit, PA: Rowman and Littlefield Publishers, Inc.

Manski, Charles F.
1999. Identification Problems in the Social Sciences. Cambridge, MA: Harvard University Press.

Nolan, Riall
(in press; available March 2003). Directions in Applied Anthropology. Boulder, CO: Lynne Rienner Publishers.

Painter, Michael
2000. Nonacademic Experience and Changing Views of the Discipline. In Sabloff, Paula L.W. (ed.): Careers in Anthropology: Profiles of Practitioner Anthropologists (NAPA Bulletin no. 20), pp. 75-81. Washington, DC: American Anthropological Association.

Price, Laurie J.
2001. "The Mismatch Between Anthropology Graduate Training and the Work Lives of Graduates." Practicing Anthropology 23(1):55-60.

Sabloff, Paula L.W. (ed.)
2000. Careers in Anthropology: Profiles of Practitioner Anthropologists (NAPA Bulletin no. 20). Washington, DC: American Anthropological Association.

Scheper-Hughes, Nancy
1995. "The Primacy of the Ethical: Propositions for a Militant Anthropology." Current Anthropology 36(3):409-420.

Simonelli, Jeanne
2001. "Mainstreaming the Applied Track: Connections, Guides, and Concerns." Practicing Anthropology 23(1):48-49.

Society for Applied Anthropology
n.d. Guide to Training Programs in the Applications of Anthropology (a periodical publication of the SfAA). Oklahoma City, OK: Society for Applied Anthropology.

Stapp, Darby

2000. "Putting Anthropology to Work." In Sabloff, Paula L.W. (ed.): Careers in Anthropology: Profiles of Practitioner Anthropologists (NAPA Bulletin no. 20), pp. 5-7. Washington, DC: American Anthropological Association.

Stephens, W. Richard
2002. Careers in Anthropology: What an Anthropology Degree Can Do For You. Boston: Allyn and Bacon.

van Willigen, John
1987. Becoming a Practicing Anthropologist: A Guide to Careers and Training Programs in Applied Anthropology (NAPA Bulletin No. 3). Washington, DC: American Anthropological Association.

2002. Applied Anthropology: An Introduction (3rd ed). Westport, CT: Bergin and Garvey.

Walker, Christopher H.
1997. Reflections of an 'Outsider' Anthropologist. In Wallace, James M. T. (ed.): Practicing Anthropology in the South, pp. 48-53. Athens, GA: Univ. of Georgia Press.

Wallace, James M. T.
1997. "Putting Anthropology into Practice in the 1990s." In Wallace, James M.T. (ed.): Practicing Anthropology in the South, pp. 1-12. Athens, GA: Univ. of Georgia Press.

Wilson, Ruth P.
1998. "The Role of Anthropologists as Short-Term Consultants." Human Organization 57(2):245-252.

Winthrop, Robert
1997. "The Real World: Advocates, Experts, and the Art of Being Useful." Practicing Anthropology 19(3): 41-2.

Wulff, Robert M., and Shirley J. Fiske (eds.)
1987. Anthropological Praxis: Translating Knowledge into Action. Boulder, CO: Westview Press.

JOURNALS

Anthropology Today
Blackwell Publishing
350 Main St.

Malden, MA 02148
tel.: 781-388-8200
website: blackwellpublishing.com

Human Organization: Journal of the Society for Applied Anthropology
Society for Applied Anthropology
P.O. Box 2436
Oklahoma City, OK 73101-2436
tel.: 405-843-8553
email: info@sfaa.net
website: http://www.sfaa.net/ho/

NAPA Bulletin (an occasional publication of NAPA)
Publications Office
American Anthropological Association
4350 North Fairfax Drive, Suite 640
Arlington, VA 22203-1620
tel.: 703-528-1902
website: http://www.napabulletin.org

Practicing Anthropology
Society for Applied Anthropology
P.O. Box 24083
Oklahoma City, OK 73124-0083
tel.: 405-843-5113
website: http://www.sfaa.net/pa

SfAA Newsletter
Society for Applied Anthropology
P.O. Box 24083
Oklahoma City, OK 73124-0083
website: http://www.sfaa.net/

GRADUATE PROGRAMS (General Applied Anthropology)

Note: Graduate Programs focusing on a specialty area within applied anthropology are listed separately in the topical sections, below.

The University of Alaska Fairbanks offers a Master's degree program in anthropology that prepares graduates to "pursue career positions in various levels of government and business."
UAF Department of Anthropology
310 Eielson Building
P.O. Box 757720

Fairbanks, AK 99775-7720
tel.: 907-474-7288
email: fyanth@uaf.edu
website: http://www.uaf.edu/anthro/programs.html

American University offers a combined B.A./M.A. in anthropology for students with interests in several areas of applied anthropology, including social services, law, government service, or public health. Its M.A. program in Public Anthropology includes applied anthropology.

Department of Anthropology
American University
Battelle-Tompkins Room T-21
4400 Massachusetts Avenue, NW
Washington, DC 20016-8003
tel.: 202-885-1830
website: http://www.american.edu/cas/department_anthropology

The University of Arizona offers an M.A. program in Anthropology with a specialization in Applied Anthropology.

Department of Anthropology
University of Arizona
P.O. Box 210030
Tucson, AZ 85721-0030
tel.: 520-621-2585
website: w3.arizona.edu/anthro/

Boston University offers an M.A. program in Applied Anthropology, as well as Ph.D. programs in various specialty areas.

Department of Anthropology
Boston University
232 Bay State Road
Boston, MA 02215
tel.: 617-353-2195
email: oneil@bu.edu
website: http://www.bu.edu/anthrop

California State University, **Chico** offers B.A./B.S. and M.A./M.S. programs in Applied Anthropology.

Department of Anthropology
California State University, Chico
W. First and Normal Sts.
Chico, CA 95929-0400
tel.: 530-898-6192
email: anth@csuchico.edu/anth
website: http://www.csuchico.edu/anth

California State University, Fullerton offers an M.A. program that specifically supports "service learning," preparing students for careers in public service agencies.

Dept. of Anthropology
California State University, Fullerton
P.O. Box 34080
Fullerton, CA 92834-9480
tel.: 714-278-2300
website: http://www.fullerton.edu

California State University, Long Beach offers graduate work in applied anthropology leading to the M.A. degree, with specialties in several applied areas.

Department of Anthropology
California State University/Long Beach
1250 Bellflower Blvd.
Long Beach, CA 90840-1003
tel.: 310-985-5171
email: rpbrophy@csulb.edu
website: http://www.csulb.edu/projects/grad

The University of California, Berkeley offers a Ph.D. program in Social Cultural Anthropology with specializations in a number of domains of application, including linguistic anthropology, the anthropology of education, the anthropology of law, historical archaeology and material culture, museum anthropology, and development.

Department of Anthropology
207 Kroeber Hall #3710
Berkeley, CA, 94720
tel.: 510-642-3406
website: http://www.ls.berkeley.edu/dept/anth/phdsoccult.intro

The University of California, San Diego offers a Ph.D. program (only) in Anthropology, designed to provide the background and skills necessary for "the application of anthropological knowledge to contemporary problems."

Department of Anthropology
University of California, San Diego
9500 Gilman Drive
La Jolla, CA 92093-0532
tel.: 858-534-0110
website http://www.ucsd.edu

The Catholic University of America offers M.A. and Ph.D. programs including applied anthropology, medical anthropology and ecological anthropology. Many graduate students participate in research and policy institutes and agencies in Washington, DC, and abroad.

Department of Anthropology
The Catholic University of America
Washington, DC, 20064
tel.: 202-319-5080
email: cua-anthro@cua.edu
website: http://www.art-sciences.cua.edu/anth/grads.cfm

The University of Florida offers graduate programs in Anthropology leading to both the Master's and Ph.D. degrees with a specialty in applied anthropology.

Department of Anthropology
University of Florida
Gainesville, FL 32611
tel.: 352-392-2031
website: http://www.anthro.ufl.edu

Georgia State University offers a program leading to the M.A. in Anthropology with an applied anthropology track, as well as a Community and Applied Research in Anthropology (CARA) program.

Director of Graduate Studies
Department of Anthropology and Geography
Georgia State University
University Plaza
Atlanta, GA, 30303
tel.: 404-651-3232
website: http://www.monarch.gsu.edu

The University of Kansas offers M.A. and Ph.D. programs in which students can specialize in applied anthropology.

Department of Anthropology
University of Kansas
622 Fraser Hall
Lawrence, KS 66045-2110
tel.: 785-864-4103
email: kuanthro@ukans,edu
website: http://www.cc.ukans.edu/kuanth

The University of Kentucky offers graduate training emphasizing applied research and leading to both the M.A. and Ph.D. degrees. Ph.D. students may specialize in Applied Social Anthropology

Department of Anthropology

University of Kentucky
211 Lafferty Hall
Lexington, KY 40506
tel.: 859-257-2710
website: http://www.uky.edu/AS/Anthropology/graduate

The **University of Maryland** offers a program leading to the degree of Master of Applied Anthropology (M.A.A).
Department of Anthropology
University of Maryland
1111 Woods Hall
College Park, MD 20742-7415
tel.: 301-405-1423
email: anthgrad@deans.umd.edu
website: http://www.bsos.umd.edu/anth

The University of Memphis offers an M.A. degree in Anthropology with a focus on practicing anthropology in four areas: multiethnic community organization, health care delivery systems, cultural resource management, and service in archaeology.
Department of Anthropology
The University of Memphis
Memphis, TN 38152
tel.: 901-878-2080
website: http://www.people.memphis.edu/~anthropology/
email: finerman@memphis.edu

Michigan State University offers a Ph.D. program in anthropology that prepares students for careers not only in academia but also in government agencies, non-governmental organizations, non-profit foundations, and private industry. The university also offers a program leading to a Masters in the Professional Applications of Anthropology (MAPAA), which specifically prepares students for careers a practicing anthropologists in several professional areas.
Department of Anthropology
Michigan State University
354 Baker Hall
East Lansing, MI 48824-1118
tel.: 517-353-2950
email: anthropology@ssc.msu.edu
website: http://www.ssc.msu.edu/anp

Montclair State University has a five-year combined B.A.-M.A. program in practical anthropology.
Department of Anthropology

Montclair State University
427 Dickson Hall
Upper Montclair NJ 07043
tel.: 973-655-4119 .
website: http://www.chss.montclair.edu
email: brookk@mail.montclair.edu

The University of New Orleans Department of Anthropology, in
conjunction with the university's College of Urban and Public Affairs,
offers an Applied Urban Anthropology track leading to the M.S. degree in
Urban Studies.
Department of Anthropology
University of New Orleans
New Orleans, LA 70148
tel.: 504-280-6294
website: http://www.uno.edu

The State University of New York at Binghampton offers M.A. and
Ph.D. degrees in cultural anthropology, emphasizing "broad training in
anthropology, especially at the Master's level."
Director of Graduate Studies
Department of Anthropology
Binghamton University
Binghamton, NY 13902-6000
tel.: 607-777-2738
email: pangolin@binghamton.edu

The University of North Texas offers a program leading to the M.A.
degree in Applied Anthropology with specializations in several areas.
Institute of Anthropology
University of North Texas
410 Avenue C, Suite 330Q
P.O. Box 310409
Denton, TX 76202-0409
tel.: 940-565-2290
email: stanczyk@scs.comm.unt.edu
website: http://www.unt.edu/anthropology

Northern Arizona University offers an M.A. program in Anthropology
with a specialization in Applied Sociocultural Anthropology.
Department of Anthropology
Northern Arizona University
Box 15200
Flagstaff, AZ 86011
tel.: 520-523-3180

website: http://www.nau.edu

Oregon State University offers a program leading to an M.A. in Applied Anthropology, which provides the opportunity to specialize in one of several areas of applied anthropology.
Department of Anthropology
Oregon State University
238 Waldo Hall
Corvallis, OR97331-6403
tel.: 541-737-4515
email: jyoung@orst.edu

The University of South Florida offers programs leading to both the M.A. and Ph.D. degrees in Applied Anthropology. Areas of faculty specialization include medical anthropology, urban policy and community development, educational anthropology, cultural resources management, and economic development.
Department of Anthropology
University of South Florida
4202 E. Fowler Ave.,
Tampa, FL 33620
tel.: 813-974-2011
website: http://www.cas.usf.edu/anthropology/grad

Teachers College, Columbia University offers a program in Applied Anthropology, administered jointly with Columbia's Department of Anthropology, leading to the Ph.D. in Applied Anthropology.
Joint Program in Applied Anthropology
Columbia University, Teachers College
Department of International and Transcultural Studies
Box 19, 525 West 120th St.
New York, NY 10027
tel.: 212-678-3309
email: lc137@columbia.edu
website: http://www.tc.columbia.edu/~academic/anthro

Temple University offers programs leading to both the M.A. and Ph.D. degrees in Anthropology. Both programs broadly crosscut the four sub-disciplines of anthropology; students may choose research foci in any one of several applied areas, such as urban anthropology and medical anthropology.
Department of Anthropology
210 Gladfelter Hall
Temple University
Philadelphia PA 19122

tel.: 215-204-7577
website: anthro@blue.edu

ORGANIZATIONS

American Anthropological Association
1703 New Hampshire Ave., NW
Washington, DC 20009
tel.: 703-528-1902
website: http://www.aaanet.org

Society for Applied Anthropology (SfAA)
P.O. Box 2436
Oklahoma City, OK 73101-2436
tel.: 405-843-8553
email: info@sfaa.net
website: http://www.sfaa.net/

National Association for the Practice of Anthropology (NAPA)
c/o American Anthropological Association
1703 New Hampshire Ave., NW
Washington, DC 20009
tel.: 703-528-1902
website: http://www.aaanet.org/napa/index.htm

INFORMATIONAL WEBSITES

Anthropologists at Work: Responses to Student Questions About Anthropology Careers
http://www.anthap.oakland.edu/napafaq.htm

Anthropology in Action
http://lucy.ukc.ac.uk/Anthaction/

Anthropology Resources on the Internet
http://www.aaanet.org/resinet.htm

Anthrotech Virtual Library: Applied Anthropology
http://www.vlib.anthrotech.com/Applied-Anthropology/

The Applied Anthropology Browser
http://www.anthap.oakland.edu/browse.htm

Applied Anthropology Computer Network (ANTHAP)
http://www.anthap.oakland.edu/

Anthropologists at Work
http://www.oakland.edu/~dow/napafaq.htm

Anthropology: Education for the 21st Century
http://www.aaanet.org/sla/jla/jlamain.htm

Anthropology Index Online (the anthropological index of the Royal
Anthropological Institute; provides bibliographical references)
http://www.lucy.ukc.ac.uk/AIO.html

Anthropology in the News
http://www.tamu.edu/anthropology/news.html

Anthropology Resources on the Internet
http://www.aaanet.org/resinet.htm

AnthroTECH (a website providing anthropological resources and
services) http://www.anthrotech.com

Applied Anthropology Documentation Project
http://www.acs.oakland.edu:80/~dow/sources1.htm

Applied Anthropology on the Internet (NAPA Bulletin 19, free to NAPA
members; small charge for others)
http://www.NAPABulletin.org

Careers in Anthropology
http://www.aaanet.org/careersbroch.htm

Center for Anthropology and Science Communications
http://www.sciencesitescom.com/CASC/

National Association for the Practice of Anthropology Resource List
http://www.oakland.edu/~dow/napa/napares/napa.htm

Nicole's AnthroPage
http://www.wsu.edu/~i9248809/anthrop.html

Worldwide E-mail Directory of Anthropologists
http://www.wings.buffalo.edu/academic/department/anthropology/
weda

2. METHOD AND THEORY IN APPLIED CULTURAL ANTHROPOLOGY

SUGGESTED READINGS

Adams, William Y.
1998. The Philosophical Roots of Anthropology. Stanford, CA: Center for the Study of Language and Information.

Agar, Michael, and James MacDonald
1995. "Focus Groups and Ethnography." Human Organization 54(1):78-87.

Angrosino, Michael V.
2000. "The Culture Concept and Applied Anthropology." In Hill, Carole E., and Marietta L. Baba (eds.): The Unity of Theory and Practice in Anthropology: Rebuilding a Fractured Synthesis (NAPA Bulletin 18), pp. 67-78. Washington: National Association for the Practice of Anthropology.

Baba, Marietta L.
2000. "Theories of Practice in Anthropology: A Critical Appraisal." In Hill, Carole E., and Marietta L. Baba (eds.): The Unity of Theory and Practice in Anthropology: Rebuilding a Fractured Synthesis (NAPA Bulletin 18), pp. 17-44. Washington, DC: National Association for the Practice of Anthropology.

Beebe, James
2001. Rapid Assessment Process: An Introduction. Walnut Creek, CA: AltaMira Press.

Bennett, John
1996. "Applied Anthropology: Ideological and Conceptual Aspects." Current Anthropology 36:S23-S53.

Berk, Richard A., and Peter H. Rossi
1999. Thinking About Program Evaluation (2nd ed.). Thousand Oaks, CA: Sage.

Bernard, H. Russell
1999 (ed.) Handbook of Methods in Cultural Anthropology. Walnut Creek, CA: AltaMira Press.

2001. Research Methods in Anthropology: Qualitative and Quantitative Approaches (3rd ed.). Walnut Creek, CA: AltaMira Press.

Bickman, Leonard, and Debra J. Rog (eds.)
1998. Handbook of Applied Social Research Methods. Thousand Oaks, CA: Sage Publications.

Boone, Margaret S., and John J. Wood (eds.l)
1992. Computer Applications for Anthropologists. Belmont, CA: Wadsworth Publishing Co.

Bryant, Carol A., and Doraine F.C. Bailey
1991. "The Use of Focus Group Research in Program Development." In van Willigen, John, and Timothy L. Finan (eds.): Soundings: Rapid and Reliable Research Methods for Practicing Anthropologists, pp. 24-39. Washington, DC: American Anthropological Association.

Chelimsky, Eleanor, and William R. Sadish (eds.)
1997. Evaluation for the 21st Century: A Handbook. Thousand Oaks, CA: Sage Publications.

Denzin, Norman K., and Yvonna S. Lincoln
2000. Handbook of Qualitative Research (2nd ed.) Thousand Oaks, CA: Sage Publications.

DeMunck, Victor C., and Elias J. Sobo (eds.)
1998. Using Methods in the Field: A Practical Introduction and Casebook. Walnut Creek, CA: AltaMira Press.

DeWalt, Katheen M.
2001. Participant Observation: A Guide for Fieldworkers. Walnut Creek, CA: AltaMira Press.

Ember, Carol R., and Melvin Ember
2001. Cross-Cultural Research Methods. Walnut Creek, CA: AltaMira Press.

Emerson, Robert M.
2001. Contemporary Field Research: Perspective and Formulations (2nd ed.). Prospect Heights, IL: Waveland Press.

Erickson, Ken, and Donald Stull
1998. Doing Team Ethnography: Warnings and Advice.

Thousand Oaks CA: Sage Publications.

Erickson, Paul, with Liam D. Murphy
    1998. A History of Anthropological Theory. Peterborough, Ontario:
    Broadview Press.

Ervin, Alexander M.
    2000. Applied Anthropology: Tools and Perspectives for
    Contemporary Practice. Boston, MA: Allyn and Bacon.

Finan, Timothy J., and John van Willigen
    2002. "The Pursuit of Social Knowledge: Methodology and the
    Practice of Anthropology." In McDonald, James H.: The Applied
    Anthropology Reader, pp. 62-70. Boston: Allyn and Bacon.

Finsterbusch, Kurt, L.G. Llewellyn, and C.P. Wolf (eds.)
    1983. Social Impact Assessment Methods. Beverly Hills, CA: Sage
    Publications.

Forte, James A.
    2001. Theories for Practice. Lanham, MD: University Press of
    America.

Garcia Ruiz, Carmen
    2000. "Toolkit for Professional Anthropologists." Anthropology
    News 41(3):44-45.

Goldman, Laurence R.
    2000. Social Impact Analysis: An Applied Anthropology Manual.
    Oxford, UK: Berg Publishers.

Gordon, Raymond L.
    1998. Basic Interviewing Skills. Prospect Heights, IL: Waveland
    Press.

Greenwood, Davydd J., and Morten Levin.
    1998. Introduction to Action Research: Social Research for Social
    Change. Thousand Oaks, CA: Sage.

Grills, Scott (ed.)
    1998. Doing Ethnographic Research. Thousand Oaks, CA:
    Sage Publications.

Hackenberg, R.A., and B.H. Hackenberg
    1999. "You CAN Do Something! Forming Policy from Applied

Projects, Then and Now." Human Organization 58(1):1-15.

Handwerker, W. Penn
2001. Quick Ethnography. Walnut Creek, CA: AltaMira Press.

Harris, Marvin
1998. Theories of Culture in Postmodern Times. Walnut Creek,
CA: AltaMira Press.

Harrison, Barbara
2001. Collaborative Programs in Indigenous Communities: From
Fieldwork to Practice. Walnut Creek, CA: AltaMira Press.

Hill, Carole E., and Marietta L. Baba (eds.):
2000. The Unity of Theory and Practice in Anthropology:
Rebuilding a Fractured Synthesis (NAPA Bulletin No. 18).
Washington, DC: National Association for the Practice of
Anthropology.

Keare, Douglas H.
2001. "Learning to Clap: Reflections on Top-Down vs. Bottom-Up
Development." Human Organization 60(2):159-165.

Keefe, Susan Emley (ed.)
1989. Negotiating Ethnicity: The Impact of Anthropological Theory
and Practice (NAPA Bulletin No. 8). Washington, DC: National
Association for the Practice of Anthropology.

Kozaitis, Kathryn A.
2000. "The Rise of Anthropological Praxis." In Hill, Carole E., and
Marietta L. Baba (eds.): The Unity of Theory and Practice in
Anthropology: Rebuilding a Fractured Synthesis (NAPA
Bulletin 18), pp. 45-66. Washington, DC: National
Association for the Practice of Anthropology.

Krueger, Richard A., and Mary Anne Casey
2000. Focus Groups: A Practical Guide for Applied Research (3rd
ed.). Thousand Oaks, CA: Sage Publications.

Kutsche, Paul
1998. Field Ethnography: A Manual for Doing Cultural
Anthropology. Englewood Cliffs, NJ: Prentice Hall.

Layton, Robert

1997. An Introduction to Theory in Anthropology. New York: Cambridge University Press.

Manderson, Lenore (ed.)
1996. "Handbook and Manuals in Applied Research." Practicing Anthropology 18(3):3-40 (special issue).

Martinez-Pons, Manuel
1999. Statistics in Modern Research: Applications in the Social Sciences and Education. Lanham, MD: University Press of America.

McGee, R. Jon, and Richard L. Warms
2000. Anthropological Theory: An Introductory History (2nd ed.). Mountain View, CA: Mayfield.

McKillip, Jack
1998. "Needs Analysis: Process and Techniques." In Bickman, Leonard, and Debra J. Rog (eds.): Handbook of Applied Social Research Methods, pp. 261-284. Thousand Oaks, CA: Sage Publications.

Mitchell, J. Clyde
1984. "Social Network Data." In Roy F. Ellen (ed.): Ethnographic Research: A Guide to General Conduct, pp. 67-7. (ASA Research Methods in Social Anthropology, No. 1.) London: Academic Press.

Moore, Henrietta L.
2000. Anthropological Theory Today. Malden, MA: Blackwell.

Morgan, David L.
1997. Focus Groups as Qualitative Research (2nd ed.). Thousand Oaks, CA: Sage Publications.

Morgan, David L., and Richard A. Kreuger (eds.)
1997. The Focus Group Kit (Vols. 1-6). Thousand Oaks, CA: Sage Publications.

Patton, Michael Q.
2001. Qualitative Evaluation and Research Methods (3rd ed.). Thousand Oaks, CA: Sage Publications.

Perez, Carlos A.
1997. "Participatory Research: Implications for Applied Anthropology." Practicing Anthropology 19(3):2-7.

Poggie, John J., Jr., Billie R. DeWalt, and William W. Dressler (eds.)
1992. Anthropological Research: Process and Application.
Albany: State University of New York Press.

Rhodes, Colbert
2000. Using Statistics in the Social Sciences: A Computer Integrated Approach. Walnut Creek, CA: AltaMira Press.

Robson, Colin
2001. Real World Research: A Resource for Social Scientists and Practitioners (2nd ed.). Malden, MA: Blackwell.

Salzman, Philip Carl
2001. Understanding Culture: An Introduction to Anthropological Theory. Prospect Heights, IL: Waveland Press.

Schensul, Jean J., and Margaret D. LeCompte (eds.)
1999. Ethnographers Toolkit (Vols.1-7). Walnut Creek, CA: AltaMira Press.

Scrimshaw, Nevin S., and G.R. Gleason (eds.)
1992. Rapid Assessment Procedures: Qualitative Methodologies for Planning and Evaluation of Health-Related Programs. Boston: International Nutrition Foundation for Developing Countries.

Scott, John
2000. Social Network Analysis: A Handbook (2nd edition). Thousand Oaks, CA: Sage Publications.

Stewart, David W., and Prem N. Shamdasani
1998. "Focus Group Research: Exploration and Discovery." In Bickman, Leonard, and Debra J. Rog (eds.): Handbook of Applied Social Research Methods, pp. 505-526. Thousand Oaks, CA: Sage Publications.

Trotter, Robert T., and Jean J. Schensul
1998. "Methods in Applied Anthropology." In Bernard, H. Russell (ed.): Handbook of Methods in Cultural Anthropology, pp. 691-725. Walnut Creek, CA: AltaMira Press.

van Willigen, John
2002. Applied Anthropology: An Introduction (3rd ed.). Westport, CT: Bergin and Garvey.

van Willigen, John, and Timothy L. Finan (eds.)
1991. Soundings: Rapid and Reliable Research Methods for Practicing Anthropologists (NAPA Bulletin No. 10). Washington, DC: American Anthropological Association.

Watson, C.W. (ed.)
1999. Being There: Fieldwork in Anthropology. London: Pluto Press.

Weinberg, Darin (ed.)
2001. Qualitative Research Methods. Malden, MA: Blackwell.

Whyte, William F. (ed.)
1991. Participatory Action Research. Newbury Park, CA: Sage Publications.

Wolcott, Harry F.
1999. Ethnography: A Way of Seeing. Walnut Creek, CA: AltaMira Press.

Worthen, Blaine R., James R. Sanders, and Jody L. Fitzpatrick
1996. Program Evaluation: Alternative Approaches and Practical Guidelines (2nd ed.). Boston, MA: Addison-Wesley.

Wulff, Robert M., and Shirley J. Fiske (eds.)
1987. Anthropological Praxis: Translating Knowledge into Action. Boulder, CO: Westview Press.

JOURNALS

Note: The journals listed in Ch. 1, above, contain frequent articles on method and theory in applied anthropology.

Anthropological Theory
SAGE Publications
6 Bonhill Street
London EC2A 4PU, UK
website: http://www.sagepub.co.uk

Field Methods (formerly Cultural Anthropology Methods)
Dr. H. Russell Bernard, editor
Dept. of Anthropology
University of Florida
1112 Turlington Hall

Gainesville, FL 32606
Email: ufruss@ufl.edu

Theoretical Anthropology
Institut fur Volkerkunde
University of Vienna
Universitatsstrasse 7
A-1010 Vienna, Austria
email: theoretical.anthropology@univie.ac.at
website: http://www.univie.ac.at/voelkerkundeoretical-
anthropology

INFORMATIONAL WEBSITES

Cultural Anthropology Methods
http://www.lawrence.edu/fac/bradleyc/cam.html

Theory in Anthropology
http://www.indiana.edu/~wanthro/theory/htm

3. THE HISTORY OF APPLIED CULTURAL ANTHROPOLOGY

SUGGESTED READINGS

Adams, William Y.
1998. The Philosophical Roots of Anthropology. Stanford, CA:
Center for the Study of Language and Information.

Chambers, Erve
1989 (orig. 1985). Applied Anthropology: A Practical Guide.
Prospect Heights, IL: Waveland Press.

Des Chene, Mary
1997. "Locating the Past." In Gupta, Akhil, and James Ferguson
(eds.): Anthropological Locations: Boundaries and Grounds of a
Field Science, pp. 66-85. Berkeley: University of California Press.

Diamond, Jared
1997. Guns, Germs, and Steel: The Fates of Human Societies.
New York: W.W. Norton and Co.

Doughty, Paul L.
1987. "Vicos: Success, Rejection, and Rediscovery of a Classic
Program." In Eddy, Elizabeth M., and William L.   Partridge
(eds.): Applied Anthropology in America, 2nd ed., pp. 433-459.
New York: Columbia University Press.

Dowie, Mark
2001. American Foundations: An Investigative History.
Cambridge, MA: MIT Press.

Eddy, Elizabeth M., and William L. Partridge (eds.)
1987. Applied Anthropology in America (2nd ed.). New York:
Columbia University Press.

Erickson, Paul, with Liam D. Murphy
1998. A History of Anthropological Theory. Peterborough, Ontario:
Broadview Press.

Ervin, Alexander M.
2000. "A Brief History of Applied Anthropology." In Ervin, A.M.:
Applied Anthropology: Tools and Perspectives for Contemporary
Practice, pp. 14-26. Boston: Allyn and Bacon.

Escobar, Arturo
1995. Encountering Development: The Making and Unmaking of the Third World. Princeton, NJ: Princeton University Press.

Ferguson, James
1997. "Anthropology and its Evil Twin: 'Development' in the Constitution of a Discipline." In Cooper, Frederick, and Randall Packard (eds.): International Development and the Social Sciences, pp. 150-175. Berkeley: University of California Press.

Foster, George
1969. Applied Anthropology. Boston: Little Brown.

Gardner, Katy, and David Lewis
1996. Anthropology, Development, and the Post-Modern Challenge. London: Pluto Press.

Higgins, Patricia J., and J. Anthony Paredes.
2000. Classics of Practicing Anthropology, 1978-1998. Oklahoma City, OK: Society for Applied Anthropology.

Johnson, Barbara Rose (ed.)
1994. Who Pays the Price? The Sociocultural Context of Environmental Crisis. Washington, DC: Island Press.

Kozaitis, Kathryn A.
2000. "The Rise of Anthropological Praxis." In Hill, Carole E., and Marietta L. Baba (eds.): The Unity of Theory and Practice in Anthropology: Rebuilding a Fractured Synthesis (NAPA Bulletin 18), pp. 45-66. Washington, DC: NAPA.

Mead, Margaret
1979. "Anthropological Contributions to National Policies During and Immediately After World War II." In Goldschmidt, Walter (ed.), The Uses of Anthropology, pp. 145-158. Washington, DC: American Anthropological Association.

Painter, Michael
2000. "Nonacademic Experience and Changing Views of the Discipline." In Sabloff, Paula L.W. (ed.): Careers in Anthropology: Profiles of Practitioner Anthropologists (NAPA Bulletin no. 20), pp. 75-81. Washington, DC: American Anthropological Association.

Pels, Peter, and Oscar Salemink (eds.)

1999. Colonial Subjects: Essays on the Practical History of
Anthropology. Ann Arbor: University of Michigan Press.

Stocking, George W., Jr.
1992. The Ethnographer's Magic and Other Essays in the
History of Anthropology. Madison, WI: University of Wisconsin
Press.

van Willigen, John
1993. "The Development of Applied Anthropology." In Applied
Anthropology (revised ed.), pp. 17-39. Westport, CT: Bergin and
Garvey.

JOURNALS

Note: The major American journals of applied anthropology -- Human
Organization: Journal of the Society for Applied Anthropology, Practicing
Anthropology, NAPA Bulletin, and SfAA Newsletter – contain articles on
the history of applied anthropology. They are listed under "Journals" in
Chapter 1, above.

GRADUATE PROGRAMS

Note: Students specifically interested in studying the history of applied
anthropology will find courses devoted to the subject offered at any of the
institutions listed in Chapter 1, above.

INFORMATIONAL WEBSITES

AnthroGlobe Archive
http://www.archive.anthroglobe.net

National Association for the Practice of Anthropology (NAPA)
http://www.aaanet.org/napa/index.htm

4. THE ETHICS OF APPLIED CULTURAL ANTHROPOLOGY

SUGGESTED READINGS

Note: Each issue of Anthropology News contains a column entitled "Ethical Dilemmas."

American Anthropological Association (AAA)
1971. Principles of Professional Responsibility. Washington, DC: American Anthropological Association.

1997. AAA Survey of Anthropology Ph.Ds. http://www.ameranthassn.org/97SURVEY.HTM

1998. "Code of Ethics of the American Anthropological Association." Anthropology Newsletter 39(6):19-20.

Cassell, Joan, and Sue-Ellen Jacobs (eds.)
1987. Handbook on Ethical Issues in Anthropology (AAA Special Publications No. 23). Washington, DC: American Anthropological Association.

D'Andrade, Roy
1995. "Moral Models in Anthropology." Current Anthropology 36(3):399-408.

Faden, R.R., and T.L. Beauchamp
1986. A History and Theory of Informed Consent. New York: Oxford University Press.

Fluehr-Lobban, Carolyn (ed.)
1991. Ethics and the Profession of Anthropology: Dialogue for a New Era. Philadelphia: University of Pennsylvania Press.

1994. "Informed Consent in Anthropological Research: We Are Not Exempt." Human Organization 53(1):1-9.

1998. "Ethics." In Bernard, H. Russell (ed.): Handbook of Methods in Cultural Anthropology, pp. 173-202. Walnut Creek, CA: AltaMira Press.

2002. "A Century of Ethics and Professional Anthropology." Anthropology News 43(3):20.

Gert, Bernard
    1995. "Universal Values and Professional Codes of Ethics."
    Anthropology Newsletter 36(7):30-31.

Gilbert, M. Jean, Nathaniel Tashima, and Claudia C. Fishman
    1991. "Ethics and Practicing Anthropologists' Dialogue with the
    Larger World: Considerations for the Formulation of Ethical
    Guidelines for Practicing Anthropologists." In Fluehr-Lobban,
    Carolyn: Ethics and the Profession of Anthropology, pp. 200-210.
    Philadelphia: University of Pennsylvania Press.

Handwerker, W. Penn
    1997. "Universal Human Rights and the Problem of Unbounded
    Cultural Meanings." American Anthropologist 99(4):799-809.

Irvine, Leslie
    1998. "Organizational Ethics and Fieldwork Realities: Negotiating
    Ethical Boundaries in Codependents Anonymous." In Grills, Scott
    (ed.): 1998. Doing Ethnographic Research, pp. 167-183. Thousand
    Oaks, CA: Sage Publications.

Jacobs, Sue-Ellen, and Joan Cassell (eds.)
    1987. Handbook on Ethical Issues in Anthropology (AAA Special
    Publications No. 23). Washington, DC: American Anthropological
    Association.

Jordan, Ann
    1996. "Review of the AAA Code of Ethics." Anthropology Newsletter
    37(4):17-18 (April 1996).

Jorgensen, Joseph G.
    1971. "On Ethics and Anthropology." Current Anthropology 12:
    321-334.

Krulfeld, Ruth M., and Jeffrey L. MacDonald (eds.)
    1998. Power, Ethics, and Human Rights: Studies of Refugee
    Research and Action. Blue Ridge Summit, PA: Rowan and
    Littlefield Publishers.

McNabb, Steven
    1995. "Social Research and Litigation: Good Intentions versus
    Good Ethics." Human Organization 54:331-335.

Mead, Margaret, Elliot D. Chapple and G. Gordon Brown

1949. "Report of the Committee on Ethics." <u>Human Organization</u> 8(2):20-21.

Plattner, Stuart
2002. "The Protection of Human Subjects in Anthropological Research." <u>Anthropology News</u> 43(5):22.

Ringberg, Torsten
1995. "Is Academic Anthropology Unethical?" <u>Anthropology Newsletter</u> 36(1):48.

Salmon, Merrilee H.
2001 (orig. 1997). "Ethical Considerations in Anthropology and Archaeology, or Relativism and Justice for All." In Endicott, Kirk M., and Robert Welsch (eds.): <u>Taking Sides: Clashing Views on Controversial Issues in Anthropology</u>, pp. 362-370. Guilford, CT: McGraw-Hill/Dushkin.

Scheper-Hughes, Nancy
1995. "The Primacy of the Ethical: Propositions for a Militant Anthropology." <u>Current Anthropology</u> 36(3):409-420.

Sieber, Joan E.
1998. "Planning Ethically Responsible Research." In Bickman, Leonard, and Debra J. Rog (eds.): <u>Handbook of Applied Social Research Methods</u>, pp 127-156. Thousand Oaks, CA: Sage Publications.

Society for Applied Anthropology
1983. "Professional and Ethical Responsibilities." In Fluehr-Lobban, Carolyn, 1991 (ed.): <u>Ethics and the Profession of Anthropology: Dialogue for a New Era</u>, Appendix F, pp. 263-264. Philadelphia: University of Pennsylvania Press.

Washburn, Wilcomb E.
1998. "What Are Anthropological Ethics?" In Wilcomb E. Washburn: <u>Against the Anthropological Grain</u>, pp. 45-62. New Brunswick, NJ: Transaction Publishers.

<u>JOURNALS</u>

<u>Business Ethics Quarterly</u>
The McDonough School of Business
Georgetown University

37th and O St., NW
Washsington, DC 20057-1147
tel.: 1-800-444-2419
website: http://www.pdcnet.org/beq.html

Criminal Justice Ethics
Institute for Criminal Justice Ethics
John Jay College of Criminal Justice
445 West 59th St.
New York, NY 10019
email: cjejj@cunyvm.cuny.edu

Ethics
University of Chicago Press, Journals Division
1427 E. 60th St.
Chicago, IL 60637
tel.: 773-702-7600
website: http://www.journals.uchicago.edu/

Journal of Mass Media Ethics
Lawrence Erlbaum Associates, Inc.
10 Industrial Ave.
Mahwah, NJ 07430-2262
website: http://www.jmme.byu.edu/

Journal of Medical Ethics (available in print and on-line)
BMJ Publishing Group
BMA House
Tavistock Square
London WC1H 9JR, U.K.
tel.: 44-(0)-20-7383-6270
email: rcostr@bmjgroup.com
website:http://www.jme.bmjjournals.com

GRADUATE PROGRAMS

Note: see http://www.ajobonline.com/gra_program.php or
http://www.gradschools.com/listings/menus/ethics_menu.html for
comprehensive lists of graduate programs in bioethics.

Note: see http://www.cep.unt.edu/other.html for a list of graduate
programs in environmental ethics.

Note: see http://www.businessethics.ca/ for a list of resources pertaining to business ethics.

Cleveland State University, through its Philosophy Department, offers a program intended mainly for professionals involved in health care practice, research, administration, or litigation, leading to a Certificate in Bioethics.
Department of Philosophy
Cleveland State University
2121 Euclid Ave.
Cleveland, OH 44115
tel.: 216-687-3900
website: http://www.csuohio.edu

The University of Nevada, Las Vegas offers a degree program leading to the M.A. in Ethics and Policy Studies.
Ethics and Policy Studies
University of Nevada, Las Vegas
Las Vegas, NV 89154-5049
tel.: 702-895-3463
website:
http://www.unlv.edu/Colleges/Graduate/degree_programs.ethics

ORGANIZATIONS

American Anthropological Association Committee on Ethics
American Anthropological Association
4350 North Fairfax Drive, Suite 640
Arlington, VA 22203-1620
tel.: 703-528-1902
website: http://www.aaanet.org

Center for Study of Ethics in the Professions (CSEP)
HUB Mezzanine, Room 204
Illinois Institute of Technology
3241 S. Federal St.
Chicago, IL 60616-3793
tel.: 312-567-3017
email: csep@iit.edu
website: http://www.iit.edu/departments/csep

Centre for Applied Ethics (CAE)
University of British Columbia
227-6356 Agricultural Road
Vancouver, BC, Canada, V6T 1Z2

tel.: 604-822-8625
email: ethics@interchange.ubc.ca
website: http://www.ethics.ubc.ca

Institute for Criminal Justice Ethics
John Jay College of Criminal Justice
445 West 59th St.
New York, NY 10019
website: http://www.lib.jjay.cuny.edu/cje/html/institute/html

Institute for Global Ethics
11 Main Street, P.O. Box 563
Camden, ME 04843
tel.: 207-236-4014
email: webethics@globalethics.org
http://www.globalethics.org

Markkula Center for Applied Ethics
Santa Clara University
500 El Camino Real
Santa Clara, CA 95053
tel.: 408-554-4000
website: http://www.scu.edu/Ethics/about/about

Office of Human Research Protections
Office of the Secretary of Health and Human Services
The Tower Building
1101 Wootton Parkway, Suite 200
Rockville, MD 20852
tel.: 301-496-7005
email: ohrp@osophs.dhhs.gov
website: http://www.ohrp.osophs.dhhs.gov

INFORMATIONAL WEBSITES

Applied Ethics Resources on HTTP://WWW
http://www.ethics.ubc.ca/resources/

Ethical Guidelines for Good Research Practice
http://www.sussex.ac.uk/Units/anthrop/ethics.html

EthicsWeb.ca (site with links to other sites on ethical concerns)
http://www.ethicsweb.ca

Federal Regulations Governing Research Involving Human Subjects:
http://www.med.umich.edu/irbmed/FederalDocuments/hhs/HHS45CF
R46.html#46.101.

Resources Library of the Institute for Criminal Justice Ethics
http://www.lib.jjay.cuny.edu/cje/html/institute/html

PART TWO:
DOMAINS OF ANTHROPOLOGICAL PRACTICE

5. DEVELOPMENT ANTHROPOLOGY

SUGGESTED READINGS: GENERAL

Adjibolosoo, Senyo (ed.)
2000. The Human Factor in Shaping the Course of History and Development. Lanham, MD: University Press of America.

Arce, Alberto, and Norman Long (eds.)
2000. Anthropology, Development, and Modernities. London: Routledge.

Bennett, John W.
1993. Human Ecology as Human Behavior: Essays in Environmental and Development Anthropology. New Brunswick, NJ: Transaction Publishers.

Black, Jan K.
1999. Development in Theory and Practice (2nd ed.). Boulder, CO: Westview Press.

Blauert, Jutta, and Simon Zadek (eds.)
1998. Mediating Sustainability: Growing Policy from the Grassroots. West Hartford, CT: Kumarian Press.

Cernea, Michael (ed.)
1985. Putting People First: Sociological Variables in Rural Development. New York: Oxford University Press.

Chambers, Robert
1983. Rural Development: Putting the Last First. New York: Longman.

Chambers, Erve
1997. Tourism and Culture: An Applied Perspective. Albany: SUNY Press.

Clarke, Mari H.
2000. "On the Road Again: International Development Consulting." In Sabloff, Paula L.W. (ed.): Careers in Anthropology: Profiles of Practitioner Anthropologists (NAPA Bulletin no. 20), pp. 71-74. Washington, DC: American Anthropological Association.

Cohen, Jeffrey H. (ed.)
2002. Economic Development: An Anthropological Approach.
Walnut Creek, CA: Altamira Press.

Cooper, Frederick, and Randall Packard (eds.)
1997. International Development and the Social Sciences.
Berkeley: University of California Press.

Crewe, Emma, and Elizabeth Harrison
1998. Whose Development? An Ethnography of Aid. London: Zed
Books.

Danesh, Abol Hassan
1999. Corridor of Hope: A Visual View of Informal Economy.
Lanham, MD: University Press of America.

de Rivero, Oscar
2001. The Myth of Development: The Non-Viable Economies of
the 21st Century. London: Zed Books.

Diamond, Jared
1997. Guns, Germs, and Steel: The Fates of Human Societies.
New York: W.W. Norton and Co.

Dorn, James A., Steve H. Hanke, and Alan A. Walters (eds.)
1998. The Revolution in Development Economics. Washington,
DC: Cato Institute.

Dudley, Eric
1993. The Critical Villager: Beyond Community Participation.
London: Routledge.

Escobar, Arturo
1991. "Anthropology and the Development Encounter: The Making
and Marketing of Development Anthropology." American
Ethnologist 18(4):16-40.

1995. Encountering Development: The Making and Unmaking of
the Third World. Princeton: Princeton University Press.

Esman, Milton J., and Ronald J. Herring (eds.)
2001. Carrots, Sticks, and Ethnic Conflict: Rethinking
Development Assistance. Ann Arbor: University of Michigan
Press.

Fall, Wendy Wilson
    2000. "Reflections on Ethics Working in International Development." In Sabloff, Paula L.W. (ed.): Careers in Anthropology: Profiles of Practitioner Anthropologists (NAPA Bulletin no. 20), pp. 82-86. Washington, DC: American Anthropological Association.

Farmer, Brian R.
    1999. The Question of Dependency and Economic Development. Blue Ridge Summit, PA: Lexington Books/Rowman and Littlefield.

Ferguson, James
    1997. "Anthropology and its Evil Twin: 'Development' in the Constitution of a Discipline." In Cooper, Frederick, and Randall Packard (eds.): International Development and the Social Sciences, pp. 150-175. Berkeley: University of California Press.

Fisher, Julie
    1997. Nongovernments: NGOs and the Political Development of the Third World. West Hartford, CT: Kumarian Press.

Gardner, Katy, and David Lewis
    1996. Anthropology, Development, and the Post-Modern Challenge. London: Pluto Press.

Grillo, Ralph, and Alan Rew (eds.)
    1985. Social Anthropology and Development Policy. London: Tavistock Publications.

Harries-Jones, Peter
    1992. "Sustainable Anthropology: Ecology and Anthropology in the Future." In Wallman, Sandra (ed.): Contemporary Futures: Perspectives from Social Anthropology, pp. 157-171. London: Routledge.

Harris, Jonathan (ed.)
    2000. Rethinking Sustainability: Power, Knowledge, and Institututions. Ann Arbor: University of Michigan Press.

Henderson, Hazel
    1999. Beyond Globalization: Shaping a Sustainable Global Economy. West Hartford, CT: Kumarian Press.

Hoy, Paula

1998. Players and Issues in International Aid. West Hartford, CT: Kumarian Press.

Inda, Jonathan Xavier, and Renato Rosaldo (eds.)
2001. The Anthropology of Globalization: A Reader. Malden, MA: Blackwell.

Johnston, Barbara Rose
1994. Who Pays the Price? Washington, DC: Island Press.

Kamarah, Umar I.
2001. Sustainable Rural Development: Semantics or Substance? The Study of Rural Projects in North Western Sierra Leone (1985-1995). Lanham, MD: University Press of America.

Keare, Douglas H.
2001. "Learning to Clap: Reflections on Top-Down vs. Bottom-Up Development." Human Organization 60(2):159-165.

Khor, Martin, and Lim Li Lin (eds.)
2001. Good Practices and Innovative Experiences in the South (series). London: Zed Books.

Koehn, Peter H., and Olatunde J.B. Ojo (eds.)
1999. Making Aid Work: Innovative Approaches for Africa at the Turn of the Century. Lanham, MD: University Press of America

Krishna, Anirudh, Norman Uphoff, and Milton J. Esman (eds.)
1996. Reasons for Hope: Instructive Expriences in Rural Development. West Hartford, CT: Kumarian Press.

1998. Reasons for Success: Learning from Instructive Experiences in Rural Development. West Hartford, CT: Kumarian Press.

Lechner, Frank, and John Boli (eds.)
1999. The Globalization Reader. Malden, MA: Blackwell.

Lempert, David H., Kim McCarthy, and Craig Mitchell
1995. A Model Development Plan: New Strategies and Perspectives. Westport, CT: Praeger.

Loker, William M. (ed.)
1999. Globalization and the Rural Poor in Latin America. Boulder, CO: Lynne Rienner Publishers.

Luce, Randall C.
1990. "Anthropologists and Private, Humanitarian Aid Agencies." In Chaiken, Miriam S., and Anne K. Fleuret (eds.): Social Change and Applied Anthropology: Essays in Honor of David W. Brokensha, pp. 32-42. Boulder, CO: Westview Press.

Mathur, Hari Mohan
1989. Anthropology and Development in Traditional Societies. New Delhi: Vikas Publ. House.

McCorkle, Constance M. (ed.)
1989. The Social Sciences in International Agricultural Research. Boulder, CO: Lynne Rienner Publishers.

Middleton, Neil, and Phil O'Keefe
2001. Redefining Sustainable Development. London: Pluto Press.

Munck, Renaldo, and Denis O'Hearn (eds.)
1999. Critical Development Theory: Contributions to a New Paradigm. London: Zed Books.

Nolan, Riall
2001. Development Anthropology: Encounters in the Real World. Boulder, CO: Westview Press.

Nugent, David (ed.)
2002. Locating Capitalism in Time and Space: Global Restructurings, Politics, and Identity. Palo Alto, CA: Stanford University Press.

Panayiotopoulos, Prodromos, and Gavin Capps (eds.)
2001. World Development: An Introduction. London: Pluto Press.

Pillsbury, Barbara
1995. "Lessons Learned in International Development: How Can We Apply Them at Home?" In Cerroni-Long, E.L.: Insider Anthropology (NAPA Bulletin No. 17). Washington, DC: National Association for the Practice of Anthropology.

Pottier, Johan (ed.)
1993. Practising Development: Social Science Perspectives. London: Routledge.

Potts, David

2000. Project Planning and Analysis for Development. Boulder, CO: Lynne Rienner Publishers.

Rai, Shirin M.
2001. Gender and the Political Economy of Development. Malden, MA: Blackwell.

Rapley, John
2002. Understanding Development: Theory and Practice in the Third World (2nd ed.). Boulder, CO: Lynne Rienner Publishers.

Reed, Richard
1997. Forest Dwellers, Forest Protectors: Indigenous Models for International Development (Cultural Survival Series in Ethnicity and Change). Boston: Allyn and Bacon.

Rich, Bruce
1994. Mortgaging the Earth: The World Bank, Environmental Impoverishment, and the Crisis of Development. Boston: Beacon Press.

Rist, Gilbert
1997. The History of Development: From Western Origins to Global Faith. London: Zed Books.

Schaeffer, Robert K.
1997. Understanding Globalization: The Social Consequences of Political, Economic, and Environmental Change. Blue Ridge Summit, PA: Rowman and Littlefield Publishers.

Schech, Susanne, and Jane Haggis
2000. Culture and Development: A Critical Introduction. Malden, MA: Blackwell.

Schech, Susanne, and Jane Haggis (eds.)
2000. Development: A Cultural Studies Reader. Malden, MA: Blackwell.

Scudder, Thayer
1999. "The Emerging Global Crisis and Development Anthropology: Can We Have an Impact?" Human Organization 58(4):351-364.

Seligson, Mitchell A., and John T. Passe-Smith (eds.)

1998. Development and Underdevelopment: The Political Economy of Global Inequality (2nd ed.). Boulder, CO: Lynne Rienner Publishers.

Sharpless, John
    1997. "Population Science, Private Foundations, and Development Aid." In Cooper, Frederick, and Randall Packard (eds.): International Development and the Social Sciences, pp. 176-200. Berkeley: University of California Press.

Turner, Mark, and David Hulme
    1997. Governance, Administration and Development: Making the State Work. West Hartford, CT: Kumarian Press.

Urban Anthropology
    2000. Special Issue: "Anthropologists and NGOs." Urban Anthropology 29(2) (summer, 2000).

World Bank
    2000. World Development Indicators, 2000. Washington, DC: The World Bank.

SUGGESTED READINGS: WOMEN IN DEVELOPMENT

Bryceson, Deborah F. (ed.)
    1995. Women Wielding the Hoe: Lessons from Rural Africa for Feminist Theory and Development Practice. Oxford: Berg Publishers.

Datta, Rekha and Judith Kornberg (eds.)
    2002. Women in Developing Countries: Assessing Strategies for Empowerment. Boulder, CO: Lynne Rienner Publishers.

Duggan, L., L. Nisonoff, N. Visvanathan, and N. Wiegersma (eds.)
    1997. The Women, Gender, and Development Reader. London: Zed Books.

Jahan, Rounaq
    1995. The Elusive Agenda: Mainstreaming Women in Development. London: Zed Books.

Jiggins, Janice

1994. Changing the Boundaries: Women-Centered Perspectives on Population and the Environment. Washington, DC: Island Press.

Kardam, Nuket
1990. Bringing Women In: Women's Issues in International Development Programs. Boulder, CO: Lynne Reinner Publishers.

Moser, C.
1993. Gender Planning and Development: Theory, Practice, and Training. London: Routledge.

Nussbaum, Martha
2000. Women and Human Development: The Capabilities Approach. Cambridge: Cambridge University Press.

Nussbaum, Martha, and Jonathan Glover (eds.)
1995. Women, Culture, and Development: A Study of Human Capabilities. New York: Oxford University Press.

Pickup, Francine, with Suzanne Williams and Caroline Sweetman
2001. Ending Violence Against Women: A Challenge for Development and Humanitarian Work. Oxford, UK: Oxfam GB.

Rao, Aruna, Mary B. Anderson, and Catherine Overholt (eds.)
1991. Gender Analysis in Development Planning: A Case Book. West Hartford, CT Kumarian Press.

Razavi, S., and C. Miller
1995. From WID to GAD: Conceptual Shifts in the Women and Development Discourse (UNDP and UNRISD Occasional Paper No. 1). Geneva: UNRISD.

Scott, Catherine V.
1996. Gender and Development: Rethinking Modernization and Dependency Theory. Boulder, CO: Lynne Reinner Publishers.

Sittirak, Sinith
1998. The Daughters of Development: Women in a Changing Environment. London: Zed Books.

Spring, Anita (ed.)
2000. Women Farmers and Commercial Ventures: Increasing Food Security in Developing Countries. Boulder, CO: Lynne Rienner Publishers

Staudt, Kathleen
    1998. Policy, Politics and Gender: Women Gaining Ground. West Hartford, CT: Kumarian Press.

United Nations
    1999. 1999 World Survey on the Role of Women in Development: Globalization, Gender, and Work. New York: United Nations.

Young, Kate
    1993. Planning Development with Women: Making a World of Difference. New York: St. Martin's Press.

JOURNALS

Community Development Journal
    Journals Marketing
    Oxford University Press,
    2001 Evans Rd., Cary, NC 27513
    tel.: 919-677-0977, ext. 6686, or 800-852-7323
    email: jnl.etoc@oup.co.uk
    website: http://www.her.oupjournals.org

Gender and Development
    Taylor and Francis Journals
    4 Park Square, Milton Park
    Abingdon, Oxfordshire, OX14 4RN, UK
    tel.: 44(0) 1235 828600
    website: http://www.taylorandfrancis.com

Journal of Agrarian Change
    Blackwell Publishing
    350 Main St.
    Malden, MA 02148
    tel.: 781-388-8200
    website: http://www.blackwellpublishers.co.uk/journals/joac

Journal of Development Economics
    Elsevier Science, Ltd.
    P.O. Box 945
    New York, NY 10159-0945
    tel.: 212-633-3730 or 1-888-437-636
    email: usinfo-f@elsevier.com
    website: http://www.elsevier.com

Journal of Development Studies
    Frank Cass and Co. Ltd,
    Crown House
    47 Chase Side
    Southgate
    London N14 5BP, UK
    website: http://www.frankcass.com/jnls/jds.htm

Development (Journal of the Society for International Development)
    Via Panisperna, 207
    00184 Rome, Italy
    tel.: 39-06-4872172
    email: info@sidint.org
    website: http://www.sidint.org

World Development
    Elsevier Science, Ltd.
    P.O. Box 945
    New York, NY 10159-0945
    tel.: 212-633-3730 or 1-888-437-636
    email: usinfo-f@elsevier.com
    website: http://www.elsevier.com

GRADUATE PROGRAMS

American University offers doctoral-level training with a focus on the anthropology of development.
    Department of Anthropology
    American University
    Battelle-Tompkins Room T-21
    4400 Massachusetts Avenue, NW
    Washington, DC 20016-8003
    tel.: 202-885-1830
    website: http://www.american.edu/cas/department_anthropology

Boston University offers a Ph. D. program in Anthropology with an emphasis on development.
    Department of Anthropology
    Boston University
    232 Bay State Road
    Boston, MA 02215
    tel.: 617-353-2195
    email: oneil@bu.edu

website: http://www.bu.edu/anthrop

The University of California, Berkeley offers a Ph.D. program in Social Cultural Anthropology with specializations in a number of domains of application, including development.
Department of Anthropology
207 Kroeber Hall #3710
Berkeley, CA, 94720
tel.: 510-642-3406
website: http://www.ls.berkeley.edu/dept/anth/phdsoccult.intro

California State University/Long Beach offers a Master of Arts degree in Anthropology with an Applied Anthropology track. Issues related to development, such as urban poverty, immigrant adjustment, and ethnic relations, are among the areas emphasized. There is a regional emphasis on southern California and the Southwest.
Department of Anthropology
California State University/Long Beach
1250 Bellflower Blvd.
Long Beach, CA 90840-1003
tel.: 310-985-5171
email: rpbrophy@csulb.edu
website: http://www.csulb.edu/projects/grad

Cornell University offers a graduate minor in Conservation and Sustainable Development. Students must additionally seek a degree in a major field.
Center for the Environment
Education Program Coordinator
201 Rice Hall
Ithaca, NY 14853-5601
tel.: 607-255-7535
email: cucfe@cornell.edu
website: http://cfe.cornell.edu

The University of Kentucky offers a Ph.D. program with a specialty in Applied Social Anthropology and a concentration in Developmental Change. This program is the oldest of its kind in the country.
Department of Anthropology
University of Kentucky
211 Lafferty Hall
Lexington, KY 40506-0024
tel.: 859-257-6922
email: rwjeff@pop.uky.edu
website: http://www.uky.edu/as/anthropology/PAR

The University of Maryland offers a program leading to the degree of Master of Applied Anthropology (M.A.A) that includes a "Community, Health, and Development" specialty.

Department of Anthropology
University of Maryland
1111 Woods Hall
College Park, MD 20742-7415
tel.: 301-405-1423
email: anthgrad@deans.umd.edu
website: http://www.bsos.umd.edu/anth

McGill University offers M.A. and Ph.D. degrees with a concentration in development anthropology.

Department of Anthropology
Room 717 Stephen Leacock Building
855 Sherbrooke St., West
Montreal Quebec, Canada H3A 2T7
tel.: 514-398-4300
website: http://www.arts.mcgill.ca/programs/anthro

Michigan State University offers a degree program leading to the Masters in the Professional Applications of Anthropology (MAPAA), which specifically prepares students for careers a practicing anthropologists in several professional areas, one of which is international development. The university also offers a graduate program in international development through its College of Social Sciences.

Department of Anthropology
Michigan State University
354 Baker Hall
East Lansing, MI 48824-1118
tel.: 517-353-2950
email: anthropology@ssc.msu.edu
website: http://www.ssc.msu.edu/anp

The University of New Orleans offers an M.A. degree program in Applied Urban Anthropology, in cooperation with the university's College of Urban and Public Affairs.

Department of Anthropology
Liberal Arts Bldg.
University of New Orleans
New Orleans, LA 70148
tel.: 504-280-6294
email: cknowles@uno.edu
website: http://www.uno.edu/~cola/anthro.html

The State University of New York at Binghamton offers M.A. and Ph.D. degree programs with concentrations in Development Anthropology. The Institute for Development Anthropology (IDA) is located there.

Department of Anthropology
State University of New York at Binghamton
Binghamton, NY 13902-6000
tel.: 607-777-2737
http://www.anthro.binghamton.edu

The University of North Texas offers a program leading to the M.A. degree in Applied Anthropology with a specialization in local development issues, designed to prepare students for employment outside academia.

Institute of Anthropology
University of North Texas
410 Avenue C, Suite 330Q
P.O. Box 310409
Denton, TX 76202-0409
tel.: 940-565-2290
email: stanczyk@scs.comm.unt.edu
website: http://www.unt.edu/anthropology

Northern Arizona University offers an M.A. program in Anthropology with a specialization in Applied Sociocultural Anthropology, one element of which is International Development.

Department of Anthropology
Northern Arizona University
Box 15200
Flagstaff, AZ 86011
tel.: 520-523-3180
website: http://www.nau.edu

The University of Sussex (U.K.) offers a doctoral program in Development Studies, and Masters programs in Gender and Development and Rural Development, through its Graduate Research Centre for Culture, Development, and Environment (CDE).

Dr. Richard Wilson
Centre for Culture, Development, and Environment
University of Sussex
Falmer, Brighton, BNI 9SJ, United Kingdom
tel.: (44) 01273 678722
email: R.Wilson@sussex.ac.uk

Wayne State University offers an individually-designed M.A. concentration in Urban Applied Anthropology.
Department of Anthropology
Wayne State University
137 Manoogian Hall
906 West Warren Ave.
Detroit, MI 48202
tel.: 313-577-2935
email: ad4844@wayne.edu
website: http://www.cla.wayne.edu/anthro/index/html

ORGANIZATIONS

ActionAid
Hamlyn House
Macdonald Road
Archway
London, N19 5PG, UK
tel.: 020 7561 7561

Aga Khan Foundation U.S.A.
1901 L Street, N.W.
Suite 700
Washington, D.C. 20036
tel.: 202-293-2537
website: http://www.akfc.ca/usa

CARE
151 Ellis Street, NE
Atlanta, GA 30303-2440
tel.: 1-800-422-7385
website: http://www.care.org

Ford Foundation
320 East 43rd Street
New York, NY 10017 USA
tel: 212- 573-5000
website: http://www.fordfound.org

Institute for Development Anthropology (IDA)
99 Collier Street
P.O. Box 2207
Binghamton, NY 13902
tel.: 607-772-6244

website: http://www.devanth.org/index.htm

Institute for International Cooperation and Development
    P.O. Box 103-F
    Williamstown, MA 01267
    tel.: (413) 458-9828
    email: iicdinfo@berkshire.net
    website: http://www.iicd-volunteer.org

Institute for Sustainable Communities
    56 College Street
    Montpelier, VT 05602
    tel.: 802-229-2900
    email: isc@iscvt.org
    website: http://www.iscvt.org

International Center for Research on Women
    1717 Massachusetts Ave., NW, Suite 302
    Washington, DC 20036
    tel.: 202-797-0007
    email: info@icrw.org
    website: http://www.icrw.org

International Red Cross
    International Federation of Red Cross and Red Crescent
    Societies
    P.O. Box 372
    CH-1211 Geneva 19, Switzerland
    tel.: 41-22-730-4222
    website: http://www.ifrc.org

Oxfam America
    26 West Street
    Boston, MA 02111-1206
    tel.: 617-482-1211
    email: info@oxfamamerica.org
    website: http://www.oxfamamerica.org

Rockefeller Foundation
    420 Fifth Avenue
    New York, NY 10018-2702
    tel.: 212-869-8500
    website: http://www.rockfound.org

Save the Children

54 Wilton Road
Westport, CT 06880
tel.: 1-800-728-3843
website: http://www.savethechildren.org

Society for International Development
Via Panisperna, 207
00184 Rome, Italy
website: http://www.sidint.org
email: info@sidint.org

United Nations
One United Nations Plaza
New York, NY 10017
tel.: 212-963-4475
email: inquiries@un.org
website: http://www.un.org/

United Nations Development Programme (UNDP)
One United Nations Plaza
New York, NY 10017
tel.: 212-906-5558
website: http://www.undp.org

United States Agency for International Development (USAID)
Ronald Reagan Building
Washington, D.C. 20523-1000
tel.: 202-712-4810
website: http://www.usaid.gov

The World Bank
1818 H Street, N.W.
Washington, DC 20433
tel.: 202-473-1000
website: http://www.worldbank.org

World Neighbors
4127 NW 122 Street
Oklahoma City, OK 73120
tel.: 1-800-242-6387 or (405) 752-9700
website: info@wn.org

World Resources Institute
10 G Street, NE, Suite 800
Washington, DC 20002

tel.: 202-729-7600
website: http://www.wwri.org

Worldwatch Institute
1776 Massachusetts Ave., NW
Washington, DC 20036
tel.: 202-452-1999
email: worldwatch@worldwatch.org
http://www.worldwatch.org

INFORMATIONAL WEBSITES

Center for International Policy
http://www.us.net/cip/index.htm

Center for Strategic and International Studies
http://www.cwis.org

The Development Policy Kiosk (a non-partisan public forum)
http://www.policykiosk.com

International Development Conference
http://www.idcnews.com

International Institute for Sustainable Development (IISD)
http://www.iisd.ca

Overseas Development Student Network
http://www.igc.apc.org/odn

Rural Policy Research Institute
http://www.rupri.org

6. ADVOCACY ANTHROPOLOGY

SUGGESTED READINGS

Anciaux, Alain
2000. "International Voices: Are We Learning from History?" Practicing Anthropology 22(4):47-8.

Barbosa, Luiz C.
1999. The Brazilian Amazon Rainforest: Global Ecopolitics, Development, and Democracy. Lanham, MD: University Press of America.

Bryant, Bunyan (ed.)
1995. Environmental Justice: Issues, Policies, and Struggles. Washington, DC: Island Press.

Bryant, Bunyan, and Paul Mohai (eds.)
1992. Race and the Incidence of Environmental Hazards: A Time for Discourse. Boulder, CO: Westview Press.

Bullard, Robert D.
1992. Confronting Environmental Racism: Voices from the Grassroots. Boston: South End Press.

Bullard, Robert D. (ed.)
1994. Unequal Protection: Environmental Justice and Communities of Color. San Francisco: Sierra Club Books.

Downe, Pamela J.
1999. "Participant Advocacy and Research with Prostitutes in Costa Rica." Practicing Anthropology 21(3):21-24.

Endicott, Kirk M., and Robert Welsch (eds.)
2001. "Do Anthropologists Have a Moral Responsibility to Defend the Interests of 'Less Advantaged' Communities?" In Kirk M. Endicott and Robert Welsch (eds.): Taking Sides: Clashing Views on Contemporary Issues in Anthropology, pp. 380-401. Guilford, CT: McGraw-Hill/Dushkin.

Evans, Tony
2001. The Politics of Human Rights: A Global Perspective. London: Pluto Press.

Gardner, Katy, and David Lewis
1996. Anthropology, Development and the Post-Modern Challenge. London: Pluto Press.

Godoy, Ricardo
2001. Indians, Markets, and Rainforests: Theoretical, Comparative, and Quantitative Explorations in the Neotropics. New York: Columbia University Press.

Greaves, Tom (ed.)
1994. Intellectual Property Rights for Indigenous Peoples: A Source Book. Oklahoma City, OK: Society for Applied Anthropology.

Hastrup, Kirsten, and Peter Elass
1990. "Anthropolgical Advocacy: A Contradiction in Terms." Current Anthropology 31(3): 301-311.

Johnston, Barbara Rose
1994 (ed.). Who Pays the Price? The Sociocultural Context of Environmental Crisis. Washington, DC: Island Press.

2000. "Practicing Anthropology in the Human Rights Arena." In Sabloff, Paula L.W. (ed.): Careers in Anthropology: Profiles of Practitioner Anthropologists (NAPA Bulletin no. 20), pp. 39-44. Washington, DC: American Anthropological Association.

Johnston, Hank, and Bert Klandermans (eds.)
1995. Social Movements and Culture. Minneapolis: University of Minnesota Press.

Khor, Martin, and Lim Li Lin (eds.)
2001. Citizen Initiatives in Social Services, Popular Education and Human Rights (Vol. 3, "Good Practices and Innovative Experiences in the South"). London: Zed Books.

La Rusic, Ignatius
1990 (orig. 1985). "Reinventing the Advocacy Wheel?" In Paine, Robert (ed.): Advocacy and Anthropology: First Encounters, pp. 22-27. St. John's, Newfoundland: Memorial University of Newfoundland.

Lubkemann, Stephen C., Larry Minear, and Thomas G. Weiss (eds.)

2000. Humanitarian Action: Social Science Connections (Watson Institute Occasional Paper No. 37). Providence, RI: The Thomas J. Watson Jr. Institute for International Studies.

Magnarella, Paul J.
2000. "Human Rights of Indigenous Peoples in International Law." Anthropology News 41(4)35-6.

Maybury-Lewis, David
1990. "A Special Sort of Pleading: Anthropology at the Service of Ethnic Groups." In Paine, Robert (ed.): Advocacy and Anthropology: First Encounters, pp. 130-148. St. John's, Newfoundland: Memorial University of Newfoundland.

1997. Indigenous Peoples, Ethnic Groups, and the State. Boston, MA: Allyn and Bacon.

Medicos Sin Fronteros (Doctors Without Borders) (ed.)
2001. Reflections on Humanitarian Action: Principles, Ethics and Contradiction. London: Pluto Press.

Miller, M.
1995. State of the Peoples: A Global Human Rights Report on Societes in Danger. Boston, MA: Beacon Press and Cultural Survival, Inc.

Nader, Laura
1999. "Thinking Public Interest Anthropology, 1890s-1990s." General Anthropology 5(2):1-9.

Paine, Robert (ed.)
1990. Advocacy and Anthropology: First Encounters. St. John's, Newfoundland: Memorial University of Newfoundland.

Reed, Richard
1997. Forest Dwellers, Forest Protectors: Indigenous Models for International Development (Cultural Survival Series in Ethnicity and Change). Boston, MA: Allyn and Bacon.

Riley, Mary
2001. "T.I.G. (Topical Interest Group) for Intellectual Property Rights." SfAA Newsletter 12(2):13-14.

Shiva, Vandana
2001. Protect or Plunder? Understanding Intellectual Property

Rights. London: Zed Books.

Singer, Merrill, Elsa Huertas, and Glenn Scott
2000. "Am I My Brother's Keeper? A Case Study of the Responsibilities of Research." Human Organization 59(4):389-398.

Stevens, Stan (ed.)
1997. Conservation Through Cultural Survival: Indigenous Peoples and Protected Areas. Washington, DC: Island Press.

Thompson, Richard H.
1997. "Ethnic Minorities and the Case for Collective Rights." American Anthropologist 99(4):786-798.

Washburn, Wilcomb E.
1998. "Should Anthropologists Involve Themselves in the Politics of Individual Tribes?" In Washburn, Wilcomb E.: Against the Anthropological Grain, pp. 63-79. New Brunswick, NJ: Transaction Publishers.

Wenz, Peter S.
1988. Environmental Justice. Albany, NY: SUNY Press.

Westra, Laura, and Peter S. Wenz
1995. Faces of Environmental Racism: Confronting Issues of Global Justice. Lanham, MD: Rowan and Littlefield.

Wilson, Richard A. (ed.)
1996: Human Rights, Culture and Context: Anthropological Perspectives. London: Pluto Press.

Winthrop, Robert
1997. "The Real World: Advocates, Experts, and the Art of Being Useful." Practicing Anthropology 19(3):41-2.

JOURNALS

Indigenous Affairs
IWGIA International Secretariat
Classensgade 11E,
DK-2100
Copenhagen, Denmark
email: iwgia@iwgia.org
website: http://www.iwgia.org/subscribe/phtml

<u>Cultural Survival Quarterly</u>
215 Prospect Street
Cambridge, MA 02139
tel.: 617-441-5400
email: csinc@cs.org

GRADUATE PROGRAMS

The University of Sussex (U.K.) offers a program leading to the M.A. in Human Rights, through its Graduate Research Centre for Culture, Development, and Environment (CDE).
Dr. Richard Wilson
Centre for Culture, Development, and Environment
University of Sussex
Falmer, Brighton, BNI 9SJ, United Kingdom
tel.: (44) 01273 678722
email: R.Wilson@sussex.ac.uk

ORGANIZATIONS

Center for Economic and Social Rights
162 Montague St., 2nd Floor
Brooklyn, NY 11201
tel.: 718-237-9145
email: rights@cesr.org
website: http://www.cesr.org

Center for World Indigenous Studies
PMB 214
1001 Cooper Point Road SW, Suite 140
Olympia, WA 98502-1107
tel.: 360-754-1990
website: www.cwis.org

Coalition for Amazonian Peoples and Their Environment
1511 K St. NW, Suite 627
Washington, DC 20005
website: http://www.amazoncoalition.org (not yet operational as of August, 2002)

Cultural Survival
215 Prospect Street

Cambridge, MA 02139
tel.: 617-441-5400
email: csinc@cs.org
website: http://www.cs.org

Development Alternatives, Inc. (DAI)
7250 Woodmont Ave., Suite 200
Bethesda, MD 20814
tel.: 301-718-8699
website: http://www.dai.com

Development Group for Alternative Policies
927 Fifteenth St., NW, 4th Floor
Washington, DC 20005
tel.: 202-898-1566
email: dgap@developmentgap.org
website: http://www.developmentgap.org

Earthjustice
1625 Massachusetts Ave., NW, Suite 702
Washington, DC 20036
tel.: 202-667-4500
website: http://www.earthjustice.org

Earthwatch International
Cultural Diversity Program
680 Mount Auburn St.
P.O. Box 9014
Watertown, MA 02272
tel.: 1-800-461-0081
email: info@earthwatch.org
website: earthwatch.org

Forefront
333 7th Ave., 13th Fl.
New York, NY 10001
tel.: 212-845-5273
website: http://www.forefrontleaders.org

Institute for Community Research, Inc.
Two Hartford Square West, Suite 100
Hartford, CT, 06106-5128
tel.: 860-278-2044
website: http://www.hartnet.org/icr

International Work Group for Indigenous Affairs (IWGIA)
        Classensgade 11E
        DK 2100 Copenhagen, Denmark
        website: http://www.iwgia.org

Peace Corps
        Paul D. Coverdell Peace Corps Headquarters
        1111 20th Street, NW
        Washington, DC 20526
        tel.: 1-800-424-8580
        website: http://www.peacecorps.gov

The Rainforest Alliance
        65 Bleeker Street
        New York, NY 10012
        tel.: 212-677-1900 or 888-MY-EARTH
        website: http://www.canopy@ra.org

South and Meso American Indian Rights Center (SAIIC)
        P.O. Box 7829
        Oakland, CA 94601
        tel.: 510-534-4882
        email: indian@igc.org
        website: http://www.saiic.nativeweb.org

INFORMATIONAL WEBSITES

Aboriginal Studies
        http://www.ciolek.com/HTTP://WWWVL-Aboriginal.html

American Friends Service Committee
        http://www.afsc.org

American Near East Refugee Aid
        http://www.anera.org

U.S. Bureau of Indian Affairs
        http://www.doi.gov/bia

Center for World Indigenous Studies
        http://www.cwis.org

Human Rights and Humanitarian Assistance
        http://www.info.pit.edu/~ian/resource/human.htm

Oxfam America
http://www.oxfamamerica.org

Survival International
http://www.survival.org.uk

7. SOCIAL WORK

SUGGESTED READINGS

Balgopal, Pallassana R. (ed.)
2000. Social Work Practice with Immigrants and Refugees. New York: Columbia University Press.

Barker, Robert L.
1999. The Social Work Dictionary (4th ed.). Washington, DC: NASW Press.

Council on Social Work Education
1996. Directory of Colleges and Universities with Accredited Social Work Degree Programs. Alexandria, VA: Council on Social Work Education, Inc.

de Montigny, Gerald A.J.
1995. Social Working: An Ethnography of Front-Line Practice. Toronto: University of Toronto Press.

Doelling, Carol N.
1997. Social Work Career Development: a Handbook for Job Hunting and Career Planning. Washington, DC: National Association of Social Workers.

Dehavenon, Anna Lou
1996. There's No Place Like Home: Anthropological Perspectives on Housing and Homelessness in the United States. Westport, CT: Bergin and Garvey.

Edwards, Richard L. (ed.)
1997. Encyclopedia of Social Work (19th ed.). Washington, DC: NASW Press.

Garner, Geraldine O.
1993. Careers in Social and Rehabilitation Services. Lincolnwood, IL: VGM Career Horizons.

Garvin, Charles D., and John E. Tropman
1992. Social Work in Contemporary Society. Englewood Cliffs, NJ: Prentice Hall.

Ginsberg, Leon H.
1998. Careers in Social Work. Boston: Allyn and Bacon.

Hopps, June Gary, and Robert Morris (eds.)
2000. Social Work at the Millennium: Critical Reflections on the Future of the Profession. New York: Free Press.

Lago, C., and J. Thompson
1996. Race, Culture, and Counselling. Buckingham: Open University Press.

Lecca, Pedro J., I. Quervalu, J.V. Nunes, and H.F. Gonzales
1998. Cultural Competency in Health, Social, and Human Services: Directions for the Twenty-First Century. New York: Garland Publishing, Inc.

McPhatter, A.
1997. "Cultural Competence in Child Welfare." Journal of Policy, Practice, and Program 86(1):255-78.

Malekoff, Andrew
1997. Group Work with Adolescents: Principles and Practice. New York: The Guilford Press.

Morales, Armando T., and Bradford W. Sheafor
1992. Social Work: A Profession of Many Faces (6th ed). Boston: Allyn and Bacon.

National Association of Social Workers (NASW)
1981. "Working Statement on the Purpose of Social Work." Social Work 26(1):1-6.

Palmer, Stephen, and Pittu Laungani (eds.)
1999. Counseling in a Multicultural Society. Thousand Oaks, CA: Sage Publications.

Passaro, Joanne
1996. The Unequal Homeless: Men on the Streets, Women in Their Place. New York: Routledge.

Pederson, Paul B.
1997. Culture-Centered Counseling Interventions. Thousand Oaks, CA: Sage Publications.

Pederson, Paul B., and Allen Ivey
1993. Culture-Centered Counseling and Interviewing Skills: A Practical Guide. Westport, CT: Praeger.

Reamer, Frederic G.
1995. Social Work Values and Ethics. New York: Columbia University Press.

Russell, Andrew, and Iain R. Edgar
1998. "Research and Practice in the Anthropology of Welfare." In Edgar, Iain R., and Andrew Russell (eds.): The Anthropology of Welfare, pp. 1-15. London: Routledge.

Sue, Derald Wing, and David Sue
1999. Counseling the Culturally Different: Theory and Practice (3rd ed.). New York: John Wiley and Sons, Inc.

Wells, Carolyn Cressy, and M. Kathleen Masch
1991. Social Work Ethics Day to Day: Guidelines for Professional Practice. Prospect Heights, IL: Waveland Press.

Williams-Gray, Brenda
2001. "A Framework for Culturally Responsive Practice." In Webb, Nancy Boyd (ed.): Culturally Diverse Parent-Child and Family Relationships, pp. 55-83. New York: Columbia University Press.

JOURNALS

British Journal of Social Work
Journals Customer Services
Oxford University Press
2001 Evans Road
Cary, NC 27513
tel.: 919-677-0977, ext. 6686 or 800-852-7323
email: jnl.etoc@oup.co.uk
website: http://www3.oup.co.uk/jnls

Health and Social Work
NASW Press
750 First St., NE, Suite 700
Washington, DC 20002-4241
tel.: 202-336-8312
email: press@naswdc.org

<u>Journal of Social Work Education</u> (available online as a member benefit
of the Council on Social Work Education; see below)
website: http://www.cswe.org

<u>Research on Social Work Practice</u>
Ingenta, Inc.
44 Brattle St., 4th Floor
Cambridge, MA 02138
tel.: 617-395-4000
website: www.ingenta.com

<u>Social Work</u>
NASW Press
750 First St., NE, Suite 700
Washington, DC 20002-4241
tel.: 202-336-8312
email: press@naswdc.org

GRADUATE PROGRAMS

Note: see also Council on Social Work Education (1996): <u>Directory of
Colleges and Universities with Accredited Social Work Degree Programs</u>
(Alexandria, VA: Council on Social Work Education, Inc.).

Boston University offers a program leading to the M.A. in Applied
Anthropology, designed for non-anthropologists either currently involved
or potentially interested in a number of applied fields, one of which is
social services.
Department of Anthropology
Boston University
232 Bay State Road
Boston, MA 02215
tel.: 617-353-2195
email: oneil@bu.edu
website: http://www.bu.edu/anthrop

Loyola University, Chicago offers educational programs leading to the
degrees of Master in Social Work (with a clinical concentration in
Children and Families) and Doctor of Social Work.
Loyola University - Chicago
820 North Michigan Ave.
Chicago, IL 60611
tel.: 1-800-LOYOLA
email: loyolanow@luc.edu

website: www.luc.edu

ORGANIZATIONS

Council on Social Work Education (CWSE)
    1725 Duke St., Suite 500
    Alexandria, VA 22314-3457
    tel.: 703-683-8080
    email: info@cswe.org
    website: http://www.cswe.org

Institute for Community Research, Inc.
    Two Hartford Square West, Suite 100
    Hartford, CT, 06106-5128
    tel.: 860-278-2044
    website: http://www.hartnet.org/icr

National Association of Social Workers (NASW)
    750 First Street, NE
    Washington, DC 20002-4241
    tel.: 202-408-8600
    website: http://www.naswdc.org

INFORMATIONAL WEBSITES

U.S. Department of Health and Human Services
    http://www.dhhs.gov

U.S. Department of Housing and Urban Development
    http://www.hud.gov

8. APPLIED LEGAL ANTHROPOLOGY AND LAW ENFORCEMENT

SUGGESTED READINGS

Alexander, Jack
1988. "Working in a Prison Organization." In Hanson, Karen J.
(ed.): Mainstreaming Anthropology: Experiences in Government
Employment, pp. 16-27. Washington, DC: NAPA.

Barker, Joan C.
1999. Danger, Duty and Disillusion: The Worldview of Los
Angeles Police Officers. Prospect Heights, IL: Waveland Press.

Bouchet-Saulnier, Francoise
2001. The Practical Guide to Humanitarian Law. Blue Ridge
Summit, PA: Rowman and Littlefield Publishers, Inc.

Burton, John W.
1996. Conflict Resolution: Its Languages and Processes.
Landham, MD: Scarecrow Press.

Chamelin, Neil C.
2000. Criminal Law for Police Officers (7th ed.). Englewood Cliffs,
NJ: Prentice Hall.

Dempsey, John S.
1994. Policing: An Introduction to Law Enforcement.
Minneapolis/St. Paul, MN: West Publishing Co.

Dickerson, Debra
2000. "Cops in the 'Hood." In Fitzgerald, Terence J. (ed.): Police in
Society, pp. 63-67. New York: H.W. Wilson Co.

Dobyns, Henry F.
1987. "Taking the Witness Stand." In Eddy, Elizabeth M., and
William L. Partridge (eds.): Applied Anthropology in America (2nd
ed.), pp. 366-380. New York: Columbia University Press.

Emsley, Clive
2000. "The Origins of the Modern Police." In Fitzgerald, Terence J.
(ed.): Police in Society, pp. 9-17. New York: H.W. Wilson Co.

Erickson, Lee C.

2000. "Cooperative Policing: Bridging the Gap of Community Policing." In Fitzgerald, Terence J. (ed.): Police in Society, pp. 173-182. New York: H.W. Wilson Co.

Fitzgerald, Terence J. (ed.)
2000. Police in Society. New York: H.W. Wilson Company.

Grobsmith, Elizabeth S.
1994. Indians in Prison: Incarcerated Native Americans in Nebraska. Lincoln: University of Nebraska Press.

Heinrich, Steven A.
1993. "Commentary: Law and the Value of Anthropology." Practicing Anthropology 15(1):2,33.

Joans, Barbara
1997. "Infighting in San Francisco: Anthropology in Family Court." Practicing Anthropology 19(4):10-13.

Johansen, Bruce Elliot
1998. The Encyclopedia of Native American Legal Tradition. Westport, CT: Greenwood Press.

Kandell, Randy Frances (ed.):
1992. Double Vision: Anthropologists at Law (NAPA Bulletin No. 11). Washington, DC: National Association for the Practice of Anthropology.

Kelly, Michael J.
1996. Lives of Lawyers: Journeys in the Organizations of Practice. Ann Arbor, MI: University of Michigan Press.

La Rusic, Ignatius
1995. "Expert Witness?" In Paine, Robert: Advocacy and Anthropology, pp. 165-169. St. John's, Newfoundland: Institute of Social and Economic Research.

Lyons, William T., Jr.
1999. The Politics of Community Policing: Rearranging the Power to Punish. Ann Arbor: University of Michigan Press.

Magistro, John
1997. "An Emerging Role for Applied Anthropology: Conflict Management and Dispute Resolution." Practicing Anthropology 19(1):5-9.

Merry, Sally Engle, and Neal Milner (eds.)
1993. The Possibility of Popular Justice: A Case Study of
Community Mediation in the United States. Ann Arbor, MI:
University of Michigan Press.

Practicing Anthropology
1992. Special Issue: "Addressing Issues in Criminal Justice."
Practicing Anthropology 14(3).

Stinchcomb, Jeanne B., and Vernnon B. Fox
1998. Introduction to Corrections (5th ed.). Englewood Cliffs, NJ:
Prentice Hall.

Rohe, Willliam M., R.E. Adams, T.A. Arcury, J. Memory, and J. Klopovic
1996. Community-Oriented Policing: The North Carolina
Experience. Chapel Hill, NC: University of North Carolina Center
for Urban and Regional Studies.

Rouland, Norbert
1993. Legal Anthropology. Stanford: Stanford University Press.

Sarat, Austin, and Thomas R. Kearns (eds.)
1993. Law in Everyday Life. Ann Arbor, MI: University of Michigan
Press.

1998. Law in the Domains of Culture. Ann Arbor, MI: University of
Michigan Press.

Stinchcomb, James D.
1990. Opportunities in Law Enforcement and Criminal Justice
Careers. Lincolnwood, IL: VGM Career Horizons.

Torry, William I.
2000. "Culture and Individual Responsibility: Touchstones of the
Culture Defense." Human Organization 59(1):58-69.

Trigger, David, and Robert Blowes
2001. "Anthropologists, Lawyers, and Issues for Expert Witnesses:
Native Title Claims in Australia." Practicing Anthropology 23(1):15-
20.

Trojanowicz, Robert C., and Bonnie Bucqueroux
1990. Community Policing: A Contemporary Perspective.
Cincinnati: Anderson.

Vila, Bryan, and Cynthia Morris
1999. The Role of Police in American Society. Westport, CT: Greenwood Press.

Wolfe, Alvin W., and Honggang Yang (eds.)
1996. Anthropological Contributions to Conflict Resolution. Athens: University of Georgia Press.

Wright, Isabel
1992. "Anthropology and Capital Case Litigation." In Kandel, Randy Frances (ed.): Double Vision: Anthropologists at Law (NAPA Bulletin No. 11). Washington, DC: National Association for the Practice of Anthropology.

Yang, Honggang
1993. The Practical Use of Ethnographic Knowledge: Face-Saving Devices in Conflict Resolution. Portland, Oregon: Paper presented at the 1993 National Conference on Peacemaking and Conflict Resolution.

Young, Malcolm
1993. In the Sticks: Cultural Identity in a Rural Police Force. Oxford: Clarendon Press.

JOURNALS

Criminal Justice and Behavior
Journals Subscriptions Manager
SAGE Publications, Ltd.
6 Bonhill St.
London, EC2A 4PU, U.K.
(**Note:** also available electronically at http://www.sagepub.co.uk)

Oxford Journal of Legal Studies
Journals Marketing
Oxford University Press,
2001 Evans Rd., Cary, NC 27513
tel.: 919-677-0977, ext. 6686, or 800-852-7323
email: jnl.etoc@oup.co.uk
website: http://www.her.oupjournals.org

PoLAR (The Political and Legal Anthropology Review)
American Anthropological Association

4350 North Fairfax Drive, Suite 640
Arlington, VA 20035
tel.: 703-528-1902
website: aaanet.org/pubs

GRADUATE PROGRAMS

Note: A partial list of graduate programs in criminology, criminal justice, and related fields can be found at http://www.unl.edu/eskridge/GRADLINKS.html.

Arizona State University, through its School of Justice Studies, offers degree programs leading to the M.A. or Ph.D. program in Justice Studies.
The School of Justice Studies
Arizona State University
P.O. Box 870403
Tempe, AZ 85287-0403
tel.: 480-965-7682
email: graduate.justice@asu.edu
website: http://www.asu.edu/copp/justice/

Boston University offers a program leading to the M.A. in Applied Anthropology, designed for non-anthropologists either currently involved or potentially interested in a number of applied fields, including law.
Department of Anthropology
Boston University
232 Bay State Road
Boston, MA 02215
tel.: 617-353-2195
email: oneil@bu.edu
website: http://www.bu.edu/anthrop

The University of California, Berkeley offers a Ph.D. program in Social Cultural Anthropology with specializations in a number of domains of application, including the anthropology of law.
Department of Anthropology
207 Kroeber Hall #3710
Berkeley, CA, 94720
tel.: 510-642-3406
website: http://www.ls.berkeley.edu/dept/anth/phdsoccult.intro

The University of California, Irvine, through its School of Social Ecology's Department of Criminology, Law, and Society, offers the M.A.

in Advanced Studies in Criminology, Law, and Society and the Ph.D. in Criminology, Law, and Society.
University of California, Irvine
Social Ecology I
Irvine, CA 92697-7050
tel.: 949-824-6094
website: http://www.seweb.uci.edu/cls/

The University of Florida offers M.A. and Ph.D. programs in applied anthropology with a specialization in Legal Anthropology.
Department of Anthropology
University of Florida
Gainesville, FL 32611
tel.: 352-392-2031
website: http://www.anthro.ufl.edu

Florida State University, through its School of Criminology and Criminal Justice, offers both a Masters program (leading to either the M.S. or M.A.) and a Ph.D. program in Criminal Justice. A dual degree program in Public Administration and Criminology (M.P.A./M.Sc.) is also available through the Askew School of Public Administration and Public Policy.
School of Criminology and Criminal Justice
Florida State University
Hecht House
634 West Call St.,
Tallahassee, FL 32306
tel.: 850-644-4050
website: http://www.criminologyfsu.edu

The University of Illinois, Chicago, Department of Criminal Justice, offers programs leading to the M.A. and Ph.D. in Criminal Justice.
Department of Criminal Justice
University of Illinois at Chicago
1007 West Harrison St., M/C 141
Chicago, IL 60607
tel.: 312-996-2383
website: http://www.uic.edu/depts/cjus

Indiana University, Bloomington, through its School of Law, offers a Program for the Study of Law and Society, focusing on the intersections among criminology, political science, anthropology, and psychology. Students can earn the LLM, MCL, or SJD degrees.
Indiana University
107 S. Indiana Ave.
Bloomington, IN 47405-7000

tel.: 812-855-4848
website: http://www.law.indiana.edu/aca/lawsoc.html

John Jay College of Criminal Justice, a branch of the City University of New York, offers a program leading to the Ph.D. in Criminal Justice with an emphasis on social science methods.
John Jay College of Criminal Justice
CUNY Graduate Center
365 Fifth Ave.
New York, NY 10036
tel.: 212-817-7470
website: http://www.web.jjay.cuny.edu/~criphd/

The University of Maryland offers a program of graduate study leading to the M.A. and Ph.D. degrees in Criminology and Criminal Justice.
Graduate Program Coordinator
2220 LeFrak Hall
College Park, MD 20742
tel.: 301-405-4699
email: crimgrad@deans.umd.edu
website: http://www.bsos.umd.edu/ccjs/

The University of Missouri-St. Louis, Department of Criminology and Criminal Justice, offers courses leading to the M.A. and Ph.D. in Criminology and Criminal Justice.
Department of Criminology ajnd Criminal Justice
University of Missouri-St. Louis
324 Lucas Hall
8001 Natural Bridge Road
St. Louis, MO 63121-4499
tel.: 314-516-5031
website: http://www.umsl.edu/~ccj

Quinnipiac University, through its Center on Dispute Resolution, offers training programs for students interested in developing skills in the area of alternative dispute resolution.
Quinnipiac University Center for Dispute Resolution
275 Mount Carmel Ave.
Hamden, CT 06518
tel.: 203-582-3246
email: jennifer.brown@quinnipiac.edu
website: http://www.quinnipiac.edu/academics/law/dispute_res

ORGANIZATIONS

Academy of Criminal Justice Sciences
    7319 Hanover Parkway, Suite C
    Greenbelt, MD 20770
    tel.: 301-446-6300
    email: lmonaco@acjs.org
    website: http://www.acjs.org

Association for Political and Legal Anthropology (APLA)
    American Anthropological Association
    4350 North Fairfax Drive, Suite 640
    Arlington, VA 22203-1620
    tel.: 703-528-1902
    website: http://www.aaanet.org/apla/index.htm

American Correctional Association (ACA)
    4321 Hartwick Road
    College Park, MD 20740
    tel.: 1-800-222-5646
    website: http://www.corrections.com

American Criminal Justice Association
    P.O. Box 61047
    Sacramento, CA 95860
    tel.: 916-484-6553
    email: acjalae@aol.com
    website: http://www.acjalae.org

American Society of Criminology
    1314 Kinnear Road, Suite 212
    Columbus, OH 43212
    tel.: 614-292-9207
    website: http://www.asc41.com

Bureau of Indian Affairs (BIA)
    U.S. Department of the Interior
    1951 Constitution Ave NW
    Washington DC 20245
    tel.: 202-208-3710
    email: webmaster@bia.com (as of 8/2002, website temporarily
        unavailable)

Federal Bureau of Investigation
    Department of Justice

J. Edgar Hoover Building
935 Pennsylvania Avenue, NW
Washington, DC 20535-0001
tel.: 202-324-3000
website: http://www.fbi.gov

International Association of Chiefs of Police
515 North Washington St.
Alexandria, VA 22314
tel.: 703-836-6767 or 1-800-THE-IACP
website: http://www.theiacp.org

International Law Project for Human, Economic, and Environmental
Defense
1340 South Bonnie Brae
Los Angeles, CA 90006
tel.: 213-389-7025
email: heed@igc.org
website: http://www.heed.net

National Council on Crime and Delinquency
1970 Broadway, Suite 500
Oakland, CA 94612
tel.: 510-208-0500
email: iarifuku@sf.ncdd-crc.org
website: http://www.ndd-crc.org

National Criminal Justice Association
720 Seventh St., NW, 3rd Floor,
Washington, DC 20001-3716
tel.: 202-628-8550
email: info@ncja.org
website: http://www.ncja.org

Police Executive Research Forum (PERF)
1120 Connecticut Ave., NW,
Washington, DC 20036
tel.: 202-466-7820
website: http://www.policeforum.org

INFORMATIONAL WEBSITES

Note: See also websites for individual State Bar Associations.

AllLaw.com (comprehensive legal directory and search engine)
http://www.alllaw.com

Association for Political and Legal Anthropology (APLA)
http://www.aaanet.org/apla/index/htm

Laws.com (a compendium of legal resources available on the Web)
http://www.laws.com

Legal Links (online legal research page)
http://www.romingerlegal.com

National Criminal Justice Reference Service
http://www.ncjrs.org

Virtual Library – Law
http://www.law.indiana.edu/v-lib/

9. BUSINESS ANTHROPOLOGY

SUGGESTED READINGS

Aguilera, Francisco E.
1996. "Is Anthropology Good for the Company?" American Anthropologist 98(4):735-42.

Axtell, Roger E.
1993. Do's and Taboos Around the World. New York: John Wiley and Sons.

1997. Do's and Taboos Around the World for Women in Business. New York: John Wiley and Sons.

Baba, Marietta
1986. Business and Industrial Anthropology: An Overview (NAPA Bulletin No. 2). Washington, DC: National Association for the Practice of Anthropology.

1998. "Anthropologists in Corporate America: 'Knowledge Management' and Ethical Angst." Chronicle of Higher Education, May 8, 1998, pp. B4-5.

2000. "United Theory and Practice in American Corporations." In Sabloff, Paula L.W. (ed.): Careers in Anthropology: Profiles of Practitioner Anthropologists (NAPA Bulletin no. 20), pp. 104-106. Washington, DC: American Anthropological Association.

Benson, Judith
2000. "Challenging a Paradigm in Two Directions: Anthropologists in Business and the Business of Practicing Anthropology." In Sabloff, Paula L.W. (ed.): Careers in Anthropology: Profiles of Practitioner Anthropologists (NAPA Bulletin no. 20), pp 23-27. Washington, DC: American Anthropological Association.

Brake, Terence, Danielle Walker, and Thomas Walker
1995. Doing Business Internationally: the Guide to Cross-Cultural Success. New York: Irwin.

Brannen, Mary Yoko, and W. Mark Fruin

1999. "Cultural Alienation in Today's Multinational Work Arenas: Behavioral Fallout from Globalization." Practicing Anthropology 21(4): 20-27.

Briody, Elizabeth K., and Marietta L. Baba
1991. "Explaining Differences in Repatriation Experiences: The Discovery of Coupled and Decoupled Systems." American Anthropologist 93(2):322-344.

Burkhalter, S. Brian
1986. "The Anthropologist in Marketing." In Serrie, Hendrick, Anthropology and International Business, pp. 113-124. Williamsburg, VA: Department of Anthropology, College of William and Mary.

Davies, Lois J.
1997. "Practicing Anthropology in the Corporate World." Practicing Anthropology 19(2):30-33.

Davis, Nancy Yaw, Roger P. McConochie, and David R. Stevenson (eds.)
1987. Research and Consulting as a Business (NAPA Bulletin No. 4). Washington, DC: National Association for the Practice of Anthropology.

Ferraro, Gary
1998. Cultural Dimension of International Business (3rd ed.). Englewood Cliffs, NJ: Prentice Hall.

Garza, Christina E.
1991. "Studying the Natives on the Shop Floor." Business Week, Sept. 30, 1991: 74-78.

Giovanni, Maureen J., and Lynne M.H. Rosansky (eds.)
1990. Anthropology and Management Consulting (NAPA Bulletin No. 9). Washington, DC: National Association for the Practice of Anthropology.

Godley, Andrew, and Oliver M. Westall (eds.)
1996. Business History and Business Culture. Manchester, NY: Manchester University Press.

Gottdiener, Mark (ed.)

2000. New Forms of Consumption: Consumers, Culture, and Commodification. Lanham, MD: Rowman and Littlefield Publishers.

Hamada, Tomoko
1999. "Practicing Anthropology in Business Organizations." Practicing Anthropology 21(4):2-4.

1999 (ed.). Anthropologists and Globalization of Business Organizations. Practicing Anthropology 21(4) (special issue).

2000. "Anthropological Praxis: Theory of Business Organization. In Hill, Carole E., and Marietta L. Baba (eds.): The Unity of Theory and Practice in Anthropology: Rebuilding a Fractured Synthesis (NAPA Bulletin 18), pp. 79-103. Washington: National Association for the Practice of Anthropology.

Jones, Dell
1999. "Hot Asset in Corporate: Anthropology Degrees." USA Today, Feb. 18, 1999.

Jordan, Ann T.
1997(ed.). Practicing Anthropology in Corporate America: Consulting on Organizational Culture (NAPA Bull. No. 14). Arlington, VA: American Anthropological Association.

1999. "An Anthropological Approach to the Study of Organizational Change: The Move to Self-Managed Work Teams." Practicing Anthropology 21(4):14-19.

(forthcoming, Dec. 2002). Anthropology at Work in the Business World. Prospect Heights, IL: Waveland Press.

Kane, Kate A.
1996. "Anthropologists Go Native in the Corporate Village." FastCompany.com, Issue 5, p. 60.

Koerner, Brendan I.
1998. "Into the Wild Unknown of Workplace Culture: Anthropologists Revitalize Their Discipline." U.S. News Online, 8/10/98.

Kotter, John P.
1992. Corporate Culture and Performance. New York: Free Press.

Laabs, Jennifer J.
1992. "Corporate Anthropologists." Personnel Journal 7(1): 81-87.

Miller, Daniel
1997. Material Culture and Mass Consumerism. Malden, MA: Blackwell.

Morrison, Terri, W.A. Conaway, and G.A. Borden
1994. Kiss, Bow, and Shake Hands. Holbrook, MA: Bob Adams.

Nardi, Bonnie A.
1999. Information Ecologies: Using Technology with Heart. Cambridge, MA: M.I.T. Press.

Reeves-Ellington, Richard
1999. "From Command to Demand Economies: Bulgarian Organizational Value Orientations." Practicing Anthropology 21(4):5-13.

Rhinesmith, Stephen H.
1996. A Manager's Guide to Globalization: Six Skills for Success in a Changing World. Chicago: Irwin.

Sherry, John F., Jr. (ed.)
1995. Contemporary Marketing and Consumer Behavior: An Anthropological Sourcebook. Thousand Oaks, CA: Sage.

Squires, Susan, and Bryan Byrne (eds.)
2002. Creating Breakthrough Ideas: The Collaboration of Anthropologists and Designers in the Product Development Industry. Westport, CT: Greenwood Publishing Group.

Trice, Harrison M.
1993. Occupational Subcultures in the Workplace. Ithaca, NY: ILR Press.

Winthrop, Rob
1999. "The Real World: Words and Things." Practicing Anthropology 21(4):42-43.

JOURNALS

Competition and Change, the Journal of Global Business and Political Economy

c/o Colin Hastam
School of Management
Royal Holloway
University of London
Egham, Surry TW 20 0EX, UK
tel.: 01784 4`4350
website:http://www.gbhap.com/Competition_and_Change/

Consumption, Markets, and Culture
Taylor and Francis Journals
4 Park Square, Milton Park
Abingdon, Oxfordshire, OX14 4RN, UK
tel.: 44(0) 1235 828600
website: http://www.taylorandfrancis.com

Journal of Business Research
Elsevier Science, Ltd.
P.O. Box 945
New York, NY 10159-0945
tel.: 212-633-3730 or 1-888-437-636
email: usinfo-f@elsevier.com
website: http://www.elsevier.com

Journal of Consumer Research
University of Chicago Press.
Online edition: http://www.journals.uchicago.edu/JCR/home.html-1

Journal of Managerial Issues
Department of Economics, Finance and Banking
Pittsburgh State University
1701 S. Broadway
Pittsburg, KS 66762-7533
tel.: 316-235-4546
fax 316-235-4572
email: kbenard@pittstate.edu

Journal of Global Marketing
Erdener Kaynak, Editor-in-Chief
Journal of Global Marketing
Haworth Press
P.O. Box 399
Middletown, PA 17057
tel.: (717) 948-6343
website: http://www.haworthpressinc.com

Journal of Consumer Psychology
Dawn Iacobucci
Department of Marketing
Kellogg Graduate School of Management
Northwestern University
2001 Sheridan Road
Evanston, IL 60208
website: http://www.erlbaum.com/Journals/JCP/jcp.htm

GRADUATE PROGRAMS

The American Graduate School of International Business Management offers a degree program leading to a Masters of International Management.

Mary Teagarden, Ph.D. , Vice President for Graduate Programs
The American Graduate School of International management
Glendale, AZ
tel.: (602) 978-7392
email: teagardenm@t-bird.edu

Northwestern University, Kellogg School of Management offers a program leading to the Ph.D. degree in Marketing. Faculty interests include anthropological studies of cultural meaning.

Office of Doctoral Studies
Kellogg School of Management
Northwestern University
2001 Sheridan Road
Evanston, IL 60208-2001
tel.: 847-491-2832
website: kellogg-phd@kellogg.northwestern.edu

Oregon State University offers an M.A. program in Anthropology with a specialization in business anthropology with an Asian focus.

Department of Anthropology
Oregon State University
238 Waldo Hall
Corvallis, OR 97331-6403
tel.: 541-737-4515
email: jyoung@orst.edu

The University of South Carolina offers a Masters degree program in International Business Studies to prepare students for global business careers.

Moore School of Business
The Graduate School
University of South Carolina
Columbia, SC 29208
tel.: 803-777-4346
website: http:/mooreschool.sc.edu

Wayne State University offers an individually-designed M.A. concentration in Business and Industrial Anthropology.

Department of Anthropology
Wayne State University
137 Manoogian Hall
906 West Warren Ave.
Detroit, MI 48202
tel.: 313-577-2935
email: ad4844@wayne.edu
website: http://www.anthro.wayne.edu

The Wharton School, University of Pennsylvania offers an MBA/MA program in International Management and International Studies.

Wharton Communications
1030 Steinberg Hall-Dietrich Hall
3620 Locust Walk
Philadelphia, PA 19104
tel.: 215-898-4159
website: http://www.wharton.upenn.edu/

ORGANIZATIONS

Corporate Research International/Global Vision Institute
2400 East Main Street, Suite 103-A
St. Charles, IL 60174-2414
tel.: 630-584-5700
email: gvision@mcs.net

Intercultural Training Institute (ITI)
University of North Carolina
9201 University City Blvd
Charlotte, NC 28223-0001
tel.: (704) 687-2000
website: http://www.charweb.org/organizations/international/iti/

IOR Global Services (cross-cultural orientation resources)
    500 Skokie Blvd., Suite 600
    Northbrook, IL 60662
    tel.: 847-205-0066
    email: info@iorworld.com
    http://www.iorworld.com

ITAP International (cross-cultural consulting and training)
    268 Wall Street
    Princeton, NJ 08540
    tel.: 609-921-1446
    email itap@itapintl.com
    website: http://www.itapintlo.com/

MarketVision
    4500 Cooper Road
    Cincinnati, OH 45242
    (513) 791-3100
    website: http://www. marketvisionresearch.com

INFORMATIONAL WEBSITES

Society for the Anthropology of Work (an AAA section)
    http://www.aaanet.org/saw/index.htm

Business Culture Worldwide
    http://www.businessculture.com/

Corporateinformation (provides links to websites offering corporate
    information in over 80 countries)
    http://www.corporateinformation.com/

Corporate Intelligence II (sites for international corporate research)
    http://www.usc.edu/dept/source/intl.htm

Global Business Network
    http://www.gbn.org

Global Intercultural Services
    http://www.globalintercultural.com

Institute for Training in Intercultural Management
    http://www.itim.org/

Intercultural Business Center
http://www.ib-c.com

Intercultural Insights
http://www.egroups.com/group/interculturalinsights/info.html

WWW Virtual Library: Anthropology: Specialized Fields: Business
http://www.vlib.anthrotech.com

10. SOCIAL MARKETING

SUGGESTED READINGS

Andreason, A. R.
1995. Marketing Social Change: Changing Behavior to Promote Health, Social Development, and the Environment. San Francisco: Jossey-Bass.

1997. "Challenges for the Science and Practice of Social Marketing." In Goldberg, Marvin E., Martin Fishbein, and Susan E. Middlestadt: Social Marketing: Theoretical and Practical Perspectives, pp. 3-19. Mahwah, NJ: Lawrence Erlbaum Associates, Publishers.

2001 (ed.). Ethics in Social Marketing. Washington, DC: Georgetown University Press.

Askew, Kelly, and Richard Wilk
2002. The Anthropology of Media: A Reader. Malden, MA: Blackwell.

Auslander, Wendy, et al.
2000. "The Short-term Impact of a Health Promotion Program for Low-income African American Women." Research on Social Work Practice 10(1):78-79.

Birkinshaw, M.
1989. Social Marketing for Health. Geneva: WHO.

Black, David R., et al.
2000. "Social Marketing: Developing a Tailored Message for a Physical Activity Program." American Journal of Health Behavior 24(5):323-337.

Bracht, Neil F. (ed.)
1999. Health Promotion at the Community Level: New Advances (2nd ed.). Newbury Park, CA: Sage Publications.

Braus, Patricia
1995. "Selling Good Behavior." American Demographics 17(11): 60-64.

Breslow, Leser
1996. "Social Ecological Strategies for Promoting Healthy
Lifestyles." American Journal of Health Promotion 10(4):253-257.

Brown, Christopher A.
1997a. "Social Marketing and Applied Anthropology: A
Practitioner's View of the Similarities and Differences Between Two
Research-Driven Disciplines." In Wallace, James M.T. (ed.):
Practicing Anthropology in the South, pp., 55-64. Athens, GA:
University of Georgia Press.

1997b. "Anthropology and Social Marketing: A Powerful
Combination." Practicing Anthropology 19(4):27-29.

Campbell, Marci K., et al.
1994. "Improving Dietary Behavior: The Effectiveness of Tailored
Messages in Primary Care Settings." American Journal of Public
Health 8(5):783-787.

Cirksena, M. Kathryn, and June A. Flora
1995. "Audience Segmentation in Worksite Health Promotion: A
Procedure Using Social Marketing Concepts." Health Education
Research 10(2):211-224.

Donovan, Robert J., and Neville Owen
1994. "Social Marketing and Population Interventions." In
Dishman, Rod K. (ed.): Advances in Exercise Adherence, pp. 249-
290. Champaign, IL: Human Kinetics Publishers.

Earle, Richard
2002 (rev. ed). The Art of Cause Marketing: How to Use
Advertising to Change Personal Behavior and Public Policy. New
York: McGraw-Hill.

Fine, Seymour H.
1992. Marketing the Public Sector: Promoting the Causes of
Public and Non-Profit Agencies. Piscataway, NJ: Transaction
Publishers.

Flora, June A., Caroline Schooler and Rosalind M. Pierson
1997. "Effective Health Promotion Among Communities of Color:
The Potential of Social Marketing." In Goldberg, Marvin E., et al.:
Social Marketing: Theoretical and Practical Perspectives, pp. 353-
373. Mahwah, NJ: Lawrence Erlbaum Associates.

Freudenberg, Nicholas, *et al.*
1995. "Strengthening Individual and Community Capacity to Prevent Disease and Promote Health: In Search of Relevant Theories and Principles." Health Education Quarterly 22(3):290-306.

Glanz, Karen (ed.):
1990. Health Behavior and Health Education: Theory, Research and Practice. San Francisco: Jossey-Bass Publishers.

Goldberg, Marvin E., Martin Fishbein, and Susan Middlestadt (eds.)
1997. Social Marketing: Theoretical and Practical Perspectives. Mahwah, NJ: Lawrence Erlbaum Associates.

Hartman, Terry J., *et al.*
1997. "Results of a Community-Based Low-Literacy Nutrition Education Program." Journal of Community Health 22(5):325-341.

Harvey, Philip D.
1997. "Advertising Affordable Contraceptives: The Social Marketing Experience." In Goldberg, Marvin E., Martin Fishbein, and Susan E. Middlestadt (eds.): Social Marketing: Theoretical and Practical Perspectives, pp. 147-169. Mahwah, NJ: Lawrence Erlbaum Associates, Publishers.

1999. Let Every Child Be Wanted : How Social Marketing Is Revolutionizing Contraceptive Use Around the World. Westport, CT: Auburn House Publishers (a division of Greenwood Publishing Group).

Hofstetter, C. Richard, William A. Schultze, and Mary M. Mulvihill
1992. "Communications Media, Public Health, and Public Affairs: Exposure in a Multimedia Community." Health Communication 4(4):259-271.

Israel, Barbara A., *et al.*
1995. "Evaluation of Health Education Programs: Current Assessment and Future Directions." Health Education Quarterly 22(3):364-389.

Jackson, Lorraine D., and Bernard K. Duffy (eds.)
1998. Health Communication Research: A Guide to Developments and Directions. Westport, CT: Greenwood Press.

Kernan, Jerome B., and Teresa J. Domzal

1997. "Hippocrates to Hermes: The Postmodern Turn in Public Health Advertising." In Goldberg, Marvin E., Martin Fishbein, and Susan E. Middlestadt (eds.): Social Marketing: Theoretical and Practical Perspectives, pp. 387-416. Mahwah, NJ: Lawrence Erlbaum Associates, Publishers.

Kotler, Philip, and A. R. Andreason
1991. Strategic Marketing for Non-Profit Organizations. Englewood Cliffs, NJ: Prentice-Hall.

Kotler, Philip, and Eduardo L. Roberto
1989. Social Marketing: Strategies for Changing Public Behavior. New York: Free Press.

Kroger, Fred, et al.
1997. "Marketing Public Health: The CDC Experience." In Goldberg, Marvin E., et al., Social Marketing: Theoretical and Practical Perspectives, pp. 267-289. Mahwah, NJ: Lawrence Erlbaum Associates, Inc.

Lefebvre, Craig
1994. "Health Reform in the United States: A Social Marketing Perspective." Journal of Public Policy and Marketing 13(2):319-320.

1996. "Twenty-five Years of Social Marketing: Looking Back to the Future." Social Marketing Quarterly 3:51-58.

Lefebvre, Craig, D. Lurie, L.S. Goodman, L. Weinberg, and K. Loughrey
1995. "Social Marketing and Nutrition Education: Inappropriate or Misunderstood?" Journal of Nutrition Education 27:146-150.

Lefebvre, Craig D., L. Doner, C. Johnston, K. Loughrey, et al.
1995. "Use of Database Marketing and Cnsumer-Based Health Communication in Message Design." In Maibach, Edward, and Roxanne Louiselle Parrott (eds.): Designing Health Messages: Approaches from Communication Theory and Public Health Practice, pp. 217-246. Newbury Park, CA: Sage Publications.

Maibach, Edward, and Roxanne Louiselle Parrott (eds.)
1995. Designing Health Messages: Approaches from Communication Theory and Public Health Practice. Thousand Oaks, CA: Sage Publications.

McGrath, John C.

1991. "Evaluating National Health Communication Campaigns: Formative and Summative Research Issues." American Behavioral Scientist 34(6):652-65.

McKenzie-Mohr, Doug, and William Smith
1999. Fostering Sustainable Behavior: An Introduction to Community-Based Social Marketing. Gabriola Island, B.C., Canada: New Society Publishers.

Mintz, Jim, and Michael Steele
1992. "Marketing Health Information: The Why and How of It." Health Promotion 31(2).

Nayga, R.M., Jr.
1999. "Retail Health Marketing: Evaluating Consumers' Choice for Healthier Foods." Health Marketing Quarterly 16(4):53-65.

Niklas, Theresa A., C. Johnson, R. Farris, R. Rice, et al.
1997. "Development of a School-Based Nutrition Intervention for High School Students: Gimme 5." American Journal of Health Promotion 11(5):315-322.

Novelli, William D.
1990. "Applying Social Marketing to Health Promotion and Disease Prevention." In Glanz, Karen (ed.): Health Behavior and Health Education: Theory, Research and Practice, pp. 342-69. San Francisco: Jossey-Bass Publishers.

O'Loughlin, J.L., G. Paradis, K. Gray-Donald, and L. Renaud
1999. "The Impact of a Community-Based Heart Disease Prevention Program in a Low-Income, Inner-City Neighborhood." American Journal of Public Health 89(12):1819-26.

Orleans, C.T., J. Gruman, C. Ulmer, S.L. Emont, and J.K. Hollendonner
1999. "Rating Our Progress in Population Health Promotion: Report Card on Six Behaviors." American Journal of Health Promotion 14(2):75-82.

Pfau, Michael
1995. "Designing Messages for Behavioral Inoculation." In Maibach, Edward, and Roxanne Louiselle Parrott (eds.): Designing Health Messages: Approaches from Communication Theory and Public Health Practice, pp. 99-113. Newbury Park, CA: Sage Publications.

Rollnick, Stephen, Pip Mason, and Chris Butler
1998. Health Behavior Change: A Guide for Practitioners. Kent, UK: Churchill Livingstone.

Rudd, R.E., J. Goldberg, and W. Dietz
1999. "A Five-Stage Model for Sustaining a Community Campaign." Journal of Health Communication 4(1):37-48.

Schooler, Caroline, S.H. Chaffee, J.A. Flora, and C. Roser
1998. "Health Campaign Channels: Tradeoffs Among Reach, Specificity, and Impact." Human Communication Research 24(3):410-432.

Sherris, J.D., B.B. Ravenholt, R. Blackburn, R.H. Greenberg, N. Kak, and R.W. Porter
1985. "Contraceptive Social Marketing: Lessons from Experience." Population Reports, Series J, No. 30. Baltimore: Johns Hopkins School of Public Health, Population Information Program.

Siegel, Michael, and Lynne Doner
1998. Marketing Public Health: Strategies to Promote Social Change.
New York, NY: Aspen Publishers

Signorelli, Nancy
1998. "Health Images on Television." In Jackson, Lorraine D., and Bernard K. Duffy (eds.): Health Communication Research: A Guide to Developments and Directions, pp. 163-179. Westport, CT: Greenwood Press.

Singhal, Arvind, and Everett M. Rogers
1999. Entertainment-Education: A Communication Strategy for Social Change. Mahwah, NJ: Lawrence Erlbaum Associates.

Slater, Michael D.
1995. "Choosing Audience Segmentation Strategies and Methods for Health Communication." In Maibach, Edward, and Roxanne Louiselle Parrott (eds.): Designing Health Messages: Approaches from Communication Theory and Public Health Practice, pp. 186-198. Newbury Park, CA: Sage Publications.

Slater, Michael D., and June A. Flora
1991. "Healthy Lifestyles: Audience Segmentation Analysis for Public Health Interventions." Health Education Quarterly 18(2):221-233.

Smeltzer, Jan L., and James F. McKenzie
2000. Planning, Implementing, and Evaluating Health Promotion Programs (3rd ed.). San Francisco: Benjamin/Cummings.

Smith, William A.
1997. "Social Marketing: Beyond the Nostalgia." In Goldberg et al. (1997): Social Marketing: Theoretical and Practical Perspectives, pp. 21-28. Mahwah, NJ: Lawrence Erlbaum Associates, Publishers.

Sorensen, Glorian, et al.
1998. "The Effects of a Health Promotion – Health Protection Intervention on Behavior Change: The WellWorks Study." American Journal of Public Health 88(11):1685-90.

Stead, Martine, and Gerard Hastings
1997. "Advertising in the Social Marketing Mix: Getting the Balance Right." In Goldberg, Marvin E., et al.: Social Marketing: Theoretical and Practical Perspectives, pp. 29-43. Mahwah, NJ: Lawrence Erlbaum Associates, Publishers.

Steckler, Allan, et al.
1995. "Health Education Intervention Strategies: Recommendations for Future Research." Health Education Quarterly 22(3):307-328.

Valente, Thomas W.
2002. Evaluating Health Promotion Programs. New York: Oxford University Press.

van Willigen, John
1993. "Social Marketing." In van Willigen, John, Applied Anthroplogy: an Introduction (revised ed.), pp. 139-153. Westport, CT: Bergin and Garvey.

Walsh, Diana C., Rima E. Rudd, B.A. Moeykens and T.W. Moloney
1993. "Social Marketing for Public Health." Health Affairs 1993:104-119.

Weinreich, Nedra Kline
1999. Hands-On Social Marketing: A Step-by-Step Guide. Thousand Oaks, CA: Sage Publications.

JOURNALS

American Journal of Health Behavior
  PNG Publications
  P.O. Box 4593
  Star City, WV 26504-4593
  website: http://www.ajhb.org/subscribe2.html

American Journal of Health Promotion
  810 East 10th St.
  Lawrence, KS 66044-8897
  tel.:785-843-1235
  website: http://www.healthpromotionjournal.com

Health Education and Behavior (formerly Health Education Quarterly)
  Department of Health Behavior and Health Education
  University of Michigan, School of Public Health
  1420 Washington Heights
  Ann Arbor, MI 48109-2029
  tel.: 734-764-9494
  email: shirley.hatto@umich.edu
  website: http://www.sagepub.co.uk

Health Education Research
  Journals Marketing
  Oxford University Press,
  2001 Evans Rd., Cary, NC 27513
  tel.: 919-677-0977, ext. 6686, or 800-852-7323
  email: jnl.etoc@oup.co.uk
  website: http://www.her.oupjournals.org

Health Marketing Quarterly
  Haworth Press
  P.O. Box 399
  Middletown, PA 17057
  tel.: (717) 948-6343
  website: http://www.haworthpressinc.com

Health Promotion International (available online)
  Oxford Journals online
  website: http://www.heapro.oupjournals.org

International Quarterly of Community Health Education
  Baywood Publishing Co., Inc
  26 Austin Ave., Box 337
  Amityville, NY 11701
  tel.: 631-691-1270

email: info@baywood.lcom
website: http://www.baywood.com

Journal of Public Policy and Marketing
American Marketing Association
Warrington College of Business
Dept. of Marketing
302 Bryan Hall, P.O. Box 117155
Gainesville, Fl 32611
tel.: 352-392-0161, ext. 1232
email: jppm@cba.ufl.edu
website: http://www.marketingpower.com

Marketing Health Services (formerly Journal of Health Care Marketing)
American Marketing Association
311 S. Wacker Dr.
Chicago, IL 60606
tel.: 312-542-9000 or 1-800-AMA-1150
email: amaorders.com

Patient Education and Counseling
Elsevier Science, Ltd.
P.O. Box 945
New York, NY 10159-0945
tel.: 212-633-3730 or 1-888-437-636
email: usinfo-f@elsevier.com
website: http://www.elsevier.com

Social Marketing Quarterly
Taylor and Francis
11 New Fetter Lane
London EC4P 4EE, U.K.
tel.: 44-(0)-20-7583-9855
website http://www.tandf.co.uk/journals

GRADUATE PROGRAMS

Note: Social marketing is a component of a number of marketing
concentrations available as part of MBA programs. A comprehensive list
of such programs can be found at http://www.bus.ualberta.ca/informs.

The University of California, Davis includes the Center for Advanced
Studies in Nutrition and Social Marketing, within its Department of
Epidemiology and Preventive Medicine. The center is primarily

concerned with the uses of social marketing regarding diet and physical activity to prevent cancer and other chronic diseases in California.

Center for Advanced Studies in Nutrition and Social Marketing
Department of Epidemiology and Preventive Medicine
TB-168
University of California, Davis
One Shields Ave.
Davis, CA 95616-8638
tel.: 530-752-2793
website: http://www.socialmarketing-nutrition.ucdavis.edu

Johns Hopkins University, Bloomberg School of Public Health, offers programs leading to the MPH (Master of Public Health) as well as numerous joint degree and continuing education programs. Its Center for Communication Programs (CCP) emphasizes public health communication.

Bloomberg School of Public Health
Johns Hopkins University
615 North Wolfe St.
Baltimore, MD 21205
tel.: 410-955-5000
website: http://www.jhuccplorg

Kellogg School of Management offers a program leading to the Ph.D. degree in Marketing. Faculty interests include social marketing.

Office of Doctoral Studies
Kellogg School of Management
Northwestern University
2001 Sheridan Roa
Evanston, IL 60208-2001
tel.: 847-491-2832
website: kellogg-phd@kellogg.northwestern.edu

The University of Strathclyde, in Scotland, which houses the Centre for Social Marketing, offers the M.Sc. degree in both Marketing and International Marketing.

Department of Marketing
University of Strathclyde
Stenhouse Building
173 Cathedral Street
Glasgow, Scotland, G4 0RQ, U.K.
tel.: 44-141-548-3734
website: http://www.marketing.strath.ac.uk

ORGANIZATIONS

Academy for Educational Development
    1825 Connecticut Ave., NW
    Washington, DC 20009-5721
    tel.: 202-884-8000
    website: http://www.aed.org

Centre for Social Marketing (CSM)
    Department of Marketing
    University of Strathclyde
    Glasgow, Scotland, U.K.
    http://www.strath.ac.uk/Other/csm

Higher Education Center (technical assistance, publications, and training
    workshops in social marketing)
    Education Development Center, Inc.
    55 Chapel St.
    Newton, MA 02458-1060
    tel.: 1-800-676-1730
    email: HigherEdCtr@edc.org
    website: http://www.edc.org/hec/

The International Society for Marketing and Development (ISMD)
    c/o Erdogan Kumcu
    Dept. of Marketing
    Ball State University
    Muncie, IN 47306-0355
    tel.: 765-285-5186
    email: ismd@bsu.edu
    website: http://www.bsu.edu/xtranet/ISMD

Population Services International (a non-profit, the "leading social
    marketing organization in the world")
    1120 19th St., NW, Suite 600
    Washington, DC 20036
    tel.: 202-785-0072
    website: http:/www.psi.org

Social Marketing Institute
    1825 Connecticut Ave., NW, Suite S-852
    Washington, DC 20009
    Email: aandreas@aed.org
    website: http://www.social-marketing.org

INFORMATIONAL WEBSITES

American Marketing Association
http://www.marketingpower.com

Causemarketer.com
http://www.causemarketer.com

Health Promotion Career Network
http://www.hpcareer.net

MKT4CHANGE ("a site for social marketing")
http://www.mkt4change.com

Public Service Advertising Research Council
http://64.225.58.93/index/html

Social-Marketing.com (comprehensive on-line social marketing resources)
http://www.social-marketing.com

The Social Marketing Network
http://wwwl.hc-sc.ca/hppb/socialmarketing

Social Marketing Resources
http://www.apha.org/public_health/social.htm

Tools of Change
http://www.toolsofchange.com/English

11. APPLIED MEDICAL ANTHROPOLOGY

SUGGESTED READINGS

Baer, Hans A. (ed.)
    1987. Encounters with Biomedicine: Case Studies in Medical Anthropology. Amsterdam: Gordon and Breach.

Brown, Peter J. (ed.).
    1998. Understanding and Applying Medical Anthropology. Mountain View, CA: Mayfield.

British Medical Association
    2000. The Medical Profession and Human Rights. London: Zed Books.

Boone, Margaret S.
    1991. "Policy and Praxis in the 1990s: Anthropology and the Domestic Health Policy Arena." In Hill, Carole E. (ed.): Training Manual in Applied Medical Anthropology, pp. 23-53. Washington, DC: American Anthropological Association.

Browner, Carole H., and Carolyn F. Sargent
    1996. "Anthropology and Studies of Human Reproduction." In Sargent, Carolyn F., and Thomas M. Johnson (eds.): Handbook of Medical Anthropology: Contemporary Theory and Method (rev. ed.), pp. 219-234. Westport, CT: Greenwood Press.

Budrys, Grace
    2001. Our Unsystematic Health Care System. Blue Ridge Summit, PA: Rowman and Littlefield Publishers, Inc.

Casper, Monica J., and Barbara A. Koenig
    1996. "Reconfiguring Nature and Culture: Intersections of Medical Anthropology and Technoscience Studies." Medical Anthropology Quarterly 10(4):523-536.

Cassell, Joan
    2000. The Woman in the Surgeon's Body. Cambridge, MA: Harvard University Press.

Chrisman, Noel J., and Thomas M. Johnson
    1996. "Clinically Applied Anthropology." In Sargent, Carolyn F.,

and Thomas M. Johnson (eds.): Handbook of Medical Anthropology: Contemporary Theory and Method (rev. ed.), pp. 88-109. Westport, CT: Greenwood Press.

Chrisman, Noel J., and Thomas W. Maretzski (eds.)
1982. Clinically Applied Anthropology: Anthropologists in Health Science Settings. Boston: Kluwer Boston.

Coreil, Jeannine, and J. Dennis Mull (eds.)
1990. Anthropology and Primary Health Care. Boulder, CO: Westview Press.

Dougherty, Molly C.
1991. "Anthropologists in Nursing-Education Programs." In Hill, Carole E. (ed.): Training Manual in Applied Medical Anthropology, pp. 161-179. Washington, DC: American Anthropological Association.

Dougherty, Molly C., and Tripp-Riemer, Toni
1990. "Nursing and Anthropology." In Johnson, Thomas M., and Carolyn F. Sargent (eds.): Medical Anthropology: A Handbook of Theory and Method. Westport, CT: Greenwood Press.

Galanti, Geri-Ann
1997. Caring for Patients from Different Cultures: Case Studies from American Hospitals (2nd ed.). Philadelphia, PA: University of Pennsylvania Press.

Good, Byron J.
1994. Medicine, Rationality, and Experience: An Anthropological Perspective. Cambridge, UK: Cambridge   University Press.

Granich, Reuben, and Jonathan Mermin
1999. HIV, Health, and Your Community: a Guide for Action. Stanford, CA: Stanford University Press.

Gropper, Rena C.
1996. Culture and the Clinical Encounter: An Intellectual Sensitizer for the Health Professions. Yarmouth, ME: Intercultural Press, Inc.

Hahn, Robert A.
1995. Sickness and Healing: An Anthropological Perspective. New Haven, CT: Yale.

Helman, Cecil G.
2000. Culture, Health, and Illness (5th ed.). Oxford, UK: Butterworth-Heinemann.

Hill, Carole E. (ed.)
1991. Training Manual in Applied Medical Anthropology. Washington, DC: American Anthropological Association.

Himmelgreen, David A., et al.
2000. "Food Insecurity Among Low-Income Hispanics in Hartford, Connecticut: Implications for Public Health Policy." Human Organization 59(3):334-342.

Johnson, Thomas M.
1991. "Anthropologists in Medical Education: Ethnographic Prescriptions." In Hill, Carole E. (ed.): Training Manual in Applied Medical Anthropology, pp. 125-160. Washington, DC: American Anthropological Association.

1995. "Critical Praxis Beyond the Ivory Tower: A Critical Commentary." Medical Anthropology Quarterly 9(1):107-110.

Johnson, Thomas M., and Carolyn F. Sargent (eds.)
1990. Medical Anthropology: A Handbook of Theory and Method. Westport, CT: Greenwood Press.

Joralemon, Donald
1999. Exploring Medical Anthropology. Needham Heights, MA: Allyn and Bacon.

Lindenbaum, Shirley, and Margaret Lock (eds.)
1993. Knowledge, Power, and Practice: The Anthropology of Medicine and Everyday Life. Berkeley: University of California Press.

Loustaunau, Martha O., and Elisa Janine Sobo
1997. The Cultural Context of Health, Illness, and Medicine. Westport, CT: Bergin and Garvey.

Marshall, Patricia A.
1991. "Research Ethics in Applied Medical Anthropology." In Hill, Carole E. (ed.): Training Manual in Applied Medical Anthropology, pp. 213-235. Washington, DC: American Anthropological Association.

McElroy, Ann, and Patricia K. Townsend
1996. Medical Anthropology in Ecological Perspective (3rd ed.)
Boulder, CO: Westview Press.

Miller, Sharon Glick
1997. "The Development of Clinically Applied Anthropology: A
Cautionary Tale." In Wallace, James M.T. (ed.): Practicing
Anthropology in the South, pp. 119-126. Athens, GA: University of
Georgia Press.

Morrow, Robert C.
1997. "Anthropology in the Practice of Medicine." In Wallace,
James M.T. (ed.): Practicing Anthropology in the South, pp. 127-
132. Athens, GA: University of Georgia Press.

O'Connor, Kathleen A., and William L. Leap (eds.)
1993. "AIDS Outreach, Education, and Prevention: Anthropological
Contributions." Practicing Anthropology 15(4):3-72.

Pelto, Pertti J., and Gretel H. Pelto
1996. "Research Designs in Medical Anthropology." In Sargent,
Carolyn F., and Thomas M. Johnson (eds.): Handbook of Medical
Anthropology: Contemporary Theory and Method (rev. ed.), pp.
293-324. Westport, CT: Greenwood Press.

Pence, Gregory E.
2000. Re-creating Medicine: Ethical Issues at the Frontier of
Medicine. Lanham, MD: Rowman and Littlefield.

Romanucci-Ross, Lola, D.E. Moerman and L.R. Tancredi
1997. The Anthropology of Medicine (3rd ed.). Westport, CT: Bergin
and Garvey.

Rush, John A.
1996. Clinical Anthropology: An Application of Anthropological
Concepts Within Clinical Settings. Westport, CT: Praeger.

Sargent, Carolyn F., and Thomas M. Johnson (eds.)
1996. Handbook of Medical Anthropology: Contemporary Theory
and Method (rev. ed.). Westport, CT: Greenwood Press.

Singer, Merrill
1986. "Developing a Critical Perspective in Medical
Anthropology." Medical Anthropology Quarterly 17(9)5:128-9.

1989. "The Coming of Age of Critical Medical Anthropology." Social Science and Medicine 28:1193-1203.

1995. "Beyond the Ivory Tower: Critical Praxis in Medical Anthropology." Medical Anthropology Quarterly 9(1):80-106.

Singer, Merrill, and Hans Baer
1995. Critical Medical Anthropology. Amityville, NY: Baywood Publishing Co., Inc.

ten Brummelhuis, Han, and Gilbert Herdt (eds.)
1995: Culture and Sexual Risk: Anthropological Perspectives on AIDS. Amsterdam: Gordon and Breach Publishers.

Van Blerkom, Linda Miller
1995. "Clown Doctors: Shaman Healers of Western Medicine." Medical Anthropology Quarterly 9(4)462-475.

JOURNALS

Anthropology and Medicine (UK)
Taylor and Francis Group
11 New Fetter Lane
London EC4P 4EE, U.K.
website: http://www.tandf.co.uk/journals

Culture, Medicine and Psychiatry
Kluwer Academic/Plenum Publishers
233 Spring St.
New York, NY 10013-1578
tel.: 212-620-8014
email: teresa.krauss@wkap.com
website: http://www.kluweronline.com/issn/o165-005/current

Ethnicity and Disease
2045 Manchester St., NE
Atlanta, GA 30324
tel.: 404-875-6263
website: http://www.ishib.org/main/ed_journal.htm

Medical Anthropology: Cross Cultural Studies in Health and Illness
Department of Sociology and Anthropology
Simon Fraser University
Burnaby, British Columbia, Canada, V5A 1S6

website: http://www.sfu.ca/medanth/

Medical Anthropology Quarterly
    Mac Marshall, Editor
    Dept. of Anthropology, 114 Macbride Hall
    University of Iowa
    Iowa City, IA 52242-1322
    email: mac-marshall@uiowa.edu
    website: http://www.cudenver.edu/sma/medical_anthropology_
    quarterly

Nutritional Anthropology
    Council on Nutritional Anthropology (an AAA section)
    c/o Dr. Miriam Chaiken
    Department of Anthropology
    G12 McElhaney Hall
    Indiana University of Pennsylvania
    Indiana, PA 15705
    email: chaiken@grove.iup.edu
    website: aaanet.org/pubs/pubssubscribe.htm

Social Science and Medicine
    Elsevier Science, Ltd.
    P.O. Box 945
    New York, NY 10159-0945
    tel.: 212-633-3730 or 1-888-437-636
    email: usinfo-f@elsevier.com
    website: http://www.elsevier.com

GRADUATE PROGRAMS

Note: for an updated, comprehensive list of programs providing training in medical anthropology, go to http://www.medanth.com/programs.htm

The University of Arizona offers an M.A. program in Anthropology with a specialization in Applied Anthropology, one focus of which is Medical Anthropology.
    Department of Anthropology
    University of Arizona
    P.O. Box 210030
    Tucson, AZ 85721-0030
    tel.: 520-621-2585
    website: w3.arizona.edu/anthro/

Boston University offers a program leading to the M.A. in Applied Anthropology, designed for non-anthropologists either currently involved or potentially interested in a number of applied fields, including Medical Anthropology. There is also a Ph.D. program with an emphasis on Medical Anthropology.

Department of Anthropology
Boston University
232 Bay State Road
Boston, MA 02215
tel.: 617-353-2195
email: oneil@bu.edu
website: http://www.bu.edu/anthrop

The University of California, Berkeley offers the Ph.D. in Medical Anthropology, in cooperation with the University of California, San Francisco (see below).

Medical Anthropology
207 Kroeber Hall, #3710
Berkeley, CA 94720
tel.: 510-642-3406
website: http://www.ls.berkeley.edu/dept/anth/degrees.html

The University of California/San Francisco offers a program leading to the Ph.D. degree in Medical Anthropology (part of a joint program in medical anthropology offered by the San Francisco and Berkeley campuses of the University of California).

Department of Anthropology, History and Social Medicine
University of California/San Francisco
Box 0850
San Francisco, CA 94143-0850
tel.: 415-476-7234
email: dahsmitsa,ucsf.edu
website: http//www.ucsf.edu/dahsm

California State University/Long Beach offers a Master of Arts degree in Anthropology with an Applied Anthropology track. Medical anthropology and health care are among the areas emphasized. There is a regional emphasis on southern California and the Southwest.

Department of Anthropology
California State University/Long Beach
1250 Bellflower Blvd.
Long Beach, CA 90840-1003
tel.: 310-985-5171
email: rpbrophy@csulb.edu
website: http://www.csulb.edu/projects/grad

Case Western Reserve University offers both M.A. and Ph.D. degree programs in Medical Anthropology.
Department of Anthropology
Case Western Reserve University
10900 Euclid Ave.
Cleveland, OH 44106-7125
tel.: 216-368-2264
website: http://www.cwru.edu

The Catholic University of America offers M.A. and Ph.D. programs in medical anthropology.
Department of Anthropology
The Catholic University of America
Washington, DC, 20064
tel.: 202-319-5080
email: cua-anthro@cua.edu
website: http://www.art-sciences.cua.edu/anth/grads.cfm

The University of Connecticut offers a program, in conjunction with the Department of Community Medicine at the UConn Health Center, leading to the M.A. and Ph.D. degrees in Medical Anthropology.
Department of Anthropology
University of Connecticut
354 Mansfield Road, U-2176
Storrs, CT 06269-2176
tel.: 860-486-4512 or 860-486-2137
email: anthro@uconnvm.uconn.edu

Georgia State University offers an M.A. degree program with an applied track and a specialty in Medical Anthropology.
Georgia State University
Dept. of Anthropology and Geography
33 Gilmer St., 335 Sparks Hall
Atlanta, GA 30303
tel.: 404-651-3232
website: http://www.monarch.gsu.edu

The University of Hawaii, Manoa, Department of Anthropology, grants the M.A. and Ph.D. in Anthropology, both with a concentration in Medical Anthropology.
Department of Anthropology
University of Hawaii at Manoa
2424 Maile Way
Honolulu, Hawaii 96822

email: anthprog@hawaii.edu
website: http://www2.soc.hawaii.edu/css/anth/

The University of Kansas offers M.A. and Ph.D. programs in Anthropology that include a specialty in Medical Anthropology.

Department of Anthropology
University of Kansas
622 Fraser Hall
Lawrence, KS 66045-2110
tel.: 785-864-4103
email: kuanthro@ukans,edu
website: http://www.cc.ukans.edu/kuanth

The University of Kentucky offers a Ph.D. program with a specialty in Applied Social Anthropology and a concentration in Medical Anthropology. This program is the oldest of its kind in the U.S.

Department of Anthropology
University of Kentucky
211 Lafferty Hall
Lexington, KY 40506-0024
tel.: 859-257-6922
email: rwjeff@pop.uky.edu
website: http://www.uky.edu/as/anthropology/PAR

McGill University offers M.A. and Ph.D. degree programs with a concentration in medical anthropology.

Department of Anthropology
Room 717 Stephen Leacock Building
855 Sherbrooke St., West
Montreal Quebec, Canada H3A 2T7
tel.: 514-398-4300
website: http://www.arts.mcgill.ca/programs/anthro

The University of Memphis offers an M.A. program in Medical Anthropology, emphasizing sociocultural factors pertinent to health, addictions, nutrition, epidemiology, and treatment.

Department of Anthropology
University of Memphis
316 Manning Hall
Memphis, TN 38152-3390
tel.: 901-678-2080
email: anthropology@latte.memphis.edu
website: http://www.people.memphis.edu/anthropology

Michigan State University offers both M.A. and Ph.D. programs in Medical Anthropology.
Department of Anthropology
Michigan State University
354 Baker Hall
East Lansing, MI 48824-1118
tel.: 517-353-2950
email: anthropology@ssc.msu.edu
website: http://www.ssc.msu.edu/anp

Sarah Lawrence College incorporates a Health Advocacy Program that grants the degree of Master of Arts in Health Advocacy. The emphasis is on health care advocacy in domestic rather than international settings.
Sarah Lawrence College
1 Mead Way
Bronxville, NY 10708
tel.: 914-337-0700
email: health@mail.slc.edu
website: http://www.slc.edu

The University of South Florida offers programs leading to both the M.A. and Ph.D. degrees in Applied Anthropology. One faculty specialization is medical anthropology.
Department of Anthropology
University of South Florida
4202 E. Fowler Ave.,
Tampa, FL 33620
tel.: 813-974-2011
website: http://www.cas.usf.edu/anthropology/grad

Southern Methodist University offers a degree program leading to the M.A. in Medical Anthropology.
Southern Methodist University
Box 750336
Dallas, TX 75275-0336
tel.: 214-768-2684
website http://www2.smu.edu/anthro

The **State University of New York at Binghamton** expects, pending final approval, to offer an MS in biomedical anthropology soon.
Director of Graduate Studies
Department of Anthropology
Binghamton University
Binghamton, NY 13902-6000
tel.: 607-777-2738

email: pangolin@binghamton.edu

The State University of New York at Buffalo offers a program in Applied Medical Anthropology leading to the M.A. degree. Medical Anthropology can also be pursued at the Ph. D. level.

Department of Anthropology
State University of New York at Buffalo
380 Millard Fillmore Academic Center/Ellicott
Buffalo, NY 14261-0005
tel.: 716-645-2414
email: mal@adsu.buffalo.edu

University of North Texas grants the M.A. degree in Applied Anthropology with a specialization in Medical Anthropology. The program is specifically designed to prepare students for employment outside academia.

Institute of Anthropology
University of North Texas
410 Avenue C, Suite 330Q
P.O. Box 310409
Denton, TX 76202-0409
tel.: 940-565-2290
email: stanczyk@scs.comm.unt.edu
website: http://www.unt.edu/anthropology

Northern Arizona University offers the M.A. with a specialization in Applied Sociocultural Anthropology, one element of which is Medical Anthropology.

Department of Anthropology
Northern Arizona University
Box 15200
Flagstaff, AZ 86011
tel.: 520-523-3180
website: http://www.nau.edu

Oregon State University offers a program leading to an M.A. in Applied Anthropology, which provides the opportunity to specialize in one of several areas of applied anthropology, including health and culture,

Department of Anthropology
Oregon State University
238 Waldo Hall
Corvallis, OR 97331-6403
tel.: 541-737-4515
email: jyoung@orst.edu

Southern Methodist University offers both M.A. and Ph.D. programs in Medical Anthropology that include field internships in health care delivery systems.
Department of Anthropology
Southern Methodist University
Dallas, TX 75275-0336
tel.: 214-768-2684
email: http://www.smu.edu/~anthrop/anthmenu.html

Temple University offers programs leading to both the M.A. and Ph.D. degrees in Anthropology with a research focus in medical anthropology.
Department of Anthropology
210 Gladfelter Hall
Temple University
Philadelphia PA 19122
tel.: 215-204-7577
website: anthro@blue.edu

Wayne State University offers an M.A. degree program in anthropology with an applied medical anthropology concentration.
Department of Anthropology
Wayne State University
137 Manoogian Hall
906 West Warren Ave.
Detroit, MI 48202
tel.: 313-577-2935
email: gradvice@wayne.edu
website: http://www.cla.wayne.edu/anthro

ORGANIZATIONS

Note: Links to individual state public health associations can be found at http://www.apha.org/state_local

Council on Nursing and Anthropology (CONAA)
Nancy L.R. Anderson, President
UCLA School of Nursing
Box 956919, Factor Building 5-234
Los Angeles, CA 90095-6919
tel.: 310-206-8358
email: anderson2@ucla.edu7
website: www.conaa.org

National Institute on Drug Abuse (NIDA)
National Institutes of Health
6001 Executive Boulevard, Rm. 5213
Bethesda, MD 20892-9561
Email: information@lists.nida.nih.gov
Website: www.nida.nih.gov

The NIH Office of AIDS Research (OAR)
National Institutes of Health
Bethesda, MD 20892
tel.: 301-496-4000
email: NIHInfo@OD.NIH.gov
website: www.nih.gov/od/oar

Society for Medical Anthropology (an AAA section)
American Anthropological Association
4350 North Fairfax Drive, Suite 640
Arlington, VA 22203-1620
tel.: 703-528-1902
website: http://www.cudenver.edu/sma/index.html

INFORMATIONAL WEBSITES

Anthrotech HTTP://WWW Virtual Library: Medical Anthropology
http://www.vlib.anthrotech.com/Specialized_Fields/Medical_Anthr
opology/

Food and Agricultural Organization of the United Nations (FAO)
http://www.fao.org

Medical Anthropology Web
http://www.medanth.com

U.S. Department of Health and Human Services (DHHS)
http://www.dhhs.gov/

The Centers for Disease Control and Prevention (CDC)
http://www.cdc.gov

Causemarketer.com
http://www.causemarketer.com

U.S. National Institutes of Health
http://www.nih.gov/

12. INTERNATIONAL HEALTH

SUGGESTED READINGS

Berman, Peter, and Ravindra Rannan-Eliya
1993. Factors Affecting the Development of Private Health Care Provision in Developing Countries (Health Financing and Sustainability Project, Major Applied Research Paper No. 9). Washington, DC: USAID.

Bolton, Ralph
1995. "Rethinking Anthropology: The Study of AIDS." In ten Brummelhuis, Han, and Gilbert Herdt: Culture and Sexual Risk: Anthropological Perspectives on AIDS, pp. 285-313. Amsterdam: Gordon and Breach Publishers.

Bouvier, Leon F., and Jane T. Bertrand
1999. World Population: Challenges for the 21st Century. Santa Ana, CA: Seven Locks Press.

Bradford, Bonnie, and Margaret A. Gwynne
1995. Down to Earth: Community Perspectives on Health, Development, and the Environment. West Hartford, CT: Kumarian Press.

Coreil, Jeannine
1990. "The Evolution of Anthropology in International Health." In Coreil, Jeannine, and J. Dennis Mull (eds.): Anthropology and Primary Health Care, pp. 3-27. Boulder, CO: Westview Press.

Dixon-Mueller, Ruth
1993. Population Policy and Women's Rights: Transforming Reproductive Choice. Westport, CT: Praeger.

Forman, Shepard, and Romita Ghosh
2000. Promoting Reproductive Health: Investing in Health for Development. Boulder, CO: Lynne Rienner Publishers.

Garrett, Laurie
2000. Betrayal of Trust: The Collapse of Global Public Health. New York: Hyperion.

Hahn, Robert A. (ed.)

1999. Anthropology and Public Health: Bridging Differences in Culture and Society. New York: Oxford University Press.

Helman, Cecil G.
1994. "Medical Anthropology and Global Health." In Helman, Cecil G.: Culture, Health, and Illness (3rd ed.). Oxford, UK: Butterworth-Hienemann, Ltd.

Higginbotham, Nick, Roberto Briceno-Leon and Nancy Johnson (eds.) 2002. Applying Health Social Science: Best Practice in the Developing World. London: Zed Books.

Hill, Carole E.
1991: "Continuities and Differences in the Old and the New Applied Medical Anthropology." in Hill, Carole E. (ed.): Training Manual in Applied Medical Anthropology, pp. 14-22, Washington, DC: American Anthropological Association.

Inhorn, Marcia C., and Peter J. Brown
1998. The Anthropology of Infectious Disease: International Health Perspectives. New York: Routledge.

Kim, Jim Yong, Joyce V. Millen, Alec Irwin, and John Gershman (eds.) 2000. Dying for Growth: Global Inequality and the Health of the Poor. Monroe, ME: Common Courage Press.

Koblinsky, Marge, Judith Timyan, and Jill Gay
1993. The Health of Women: A Global Perspective. Boulder, CO: Westview Press.

Larkey, L.K., et al.
1999. "Communication Strategies for Dietary change in a Worksite Peer Educator Intervention." Health Education Research 14(6):777-790.

Lane, Sandra D., and Robert A. Rubinstein
1996. "International Health: Problems and Programs in Anthropological Perspective." In Sargent, Carolyn F., and Thomas M. Johnson (eds.): Handbook of Medical Anthropology: Contemporary Theory and Method (rev. ed.), pp. 396-423. Westport, CT: Greenwood Press.

Luckman, Joan
1999. Transcultural Communication in Health Care. Clifton Park, NY: Delmar Learning.

Macdonald, John J.
    1993. Primary Health Care: Medicine in its Place. West Hartford,
    CT: Kumarian Press.)

Moffett, George D.
    1994. Critical Masses: The Global Population Challenge. New York:
    Viking.

Nichter, Mark, and Nichter, Mimi
    1996. Anthropology and International Health: Asian Case Studies
    (2nd ed.). Amsterdam: Gordon and Breach.

Overbey, Mary Margaret
    1998. "Anthropology's Relevance to Public Health." Anthropology
    Newsletter 39(7):7.

Pillsbury, Barbara L.K.
    1991. "International Health: Overview and Opportunities." In Hill,
    Carole E. (ed.), 1991: Training Manual in Applied Medical
    Anthropology, pp. 54-87. Washington, DC: American
    Anthropological Association.

Platt, Anne
    1996. Infecting Ourselves: How Environmental and Social
    Disruptions Trigger Disease. Washington, DC: Worldwatch
    Institute.

Reid, Elizabeth (ed.)
    1995. HIV and AIDS: The Global Inter-Connection. West Hartford, CT:
    Kumarian Press.

Rockett, Ian R.H.
    1999. Population and Health: An Introduction to Epidemiology.
    Washington, DC: Population Reference Bureau.

Rodriguez-Garcia, Rosalia, and Ann Goldman (eds.)
    1994. The Health-Development Link. Washington, DC: Pan American
    Health Organization.

Sargent, Carolyn F., and Caroline B. Brettell
    1996. Gender and Health: An International Perspective.
    Englewood Cliffs, NJ: Prentice Hall.

Smeltzer, Jan L., and James F. McKenzie

2000. Planning, Implementing, and Evaluating Health Promotion Programs (3rd ed.). San Francisco: Benjamin/Cummings.

ten Brummelhuis, Han, and Gilbert Herdt
1995. Culture and Sexual Risk: Anthropological Perspectives on AIDS. Amsterdam: Gordon and Breach Publishers.

Wallace, Helen M., Kanti Giri and Carlos V. Serrano
1995. Health Care of Women and Children in Developing Countries. Oakland, CA: Third Party Publishing Co.

Whiteford, Linda M., and Lenore Manderson (eds.)
2000. Global Health Policy, Local Realities: The Fallacy of the Level Playing Field. Boulder, CO: Lynne Rienner Publishers.

Williams, Holly Ann (ed.)
2001. Caring for Those in Crisis: Integrating Anthropology and Public Health in Complex Humanitarian Emergencies (NAPA Bulletin No. 21). Washington, DC: National Association for the Practice of Anthropology.

World Health Organization (WHO)
1998. The World Health Report 1998. Geneva: World Health Organization.

JOURNALS

Evidence-Based Healthcare
Elsevier Science, Ltd.
P.O. Box 945
New York, NY 10159-0945
tel.: 212-633-3730 or 1-888-437-636
email: usinfo-f@elsevier.com
website: http://www.elsevier.com

Global AIDSLink
The Global Health Council
1701 K Street, NW
Washington, DC 20006
tel.: tel.: 202-833-5900
website: http://www.globalhealth.org

Health and Social Care in the Community
Blackwell Science Ltd.

Journal Customer Services
Osney Mead
Oxford OX2 0EL, U.K.
tel.: 44-1-1865-206180
email: jnl.orders@blacksci.co.uk
website: http://www.blackwell-science.com

Health Policy and Planning (available online)
http://www.heapol.oupjournlas.org

Health Promotion International (available online)
http://www.heapro.oupjournals.org

International Health and Human Rights (available online)
http://www.iomedcentral.com/bmcinthealthhumanrights/about

International Journal of Health Care and Quality Assurance
Elsevier Science, Ltd.
P.O. Box 945
New York, NY 10159-0945
tel.: 212-633-3730 or 1-888-437-636
email: usinfo-f@elsevier.com
website: http://www.elsevier.com

Journal of Health and Population in Developing Countries
Dept. of Health Policy and Administration
University of North Carolina
Chapel Hill, NC 27599
tel.: 919-966-7355
email: hpjournal@unc.edu

Social Science and Medicine
Elsevier Science, Ltd.
P.O. Box 945
New York, NY 10159-0945
tel.: 212-633-3730 or 1-888-437-636
email: usinfo-f@elsevier.com
website: http://www.elsevier.com

Tropical Medicine and International Health
Blackwell Science Ltd.
Journal Customer Services
Osney Mead
Oxford OX2 0EL, U.K.
tel.: 44-1-1865-206180

email: jnl.orders@blacksci.co.uk
website: http://www.blackwell-science.com

GRADUATE PROGRAMS

Note: Numerous universities in the United States and abroad offer degree programs in public health, nearly 40 of them in the U.S. alone. A list of these can be found at the website of the Association of Schools of Public Health (ASPH), http://www.asph.org.The entries below reflect programs with a specific emphasis on international public health.

Boston University offers a program leading to the M.A. in Applied Anthropology, designed for non-anthropologists either currently involved or potentially interested in a number of applied fields, including public health.

Department of Anthropology
Boston University
232 Bay State Road
Boston, MA 02215
tel.: 617-353-2195
email: oneil@bu.edu
website: http://www.bu.edu/anthrop

Boston University School of Public Health offers the Master of Public Health (MPH) degree, from which students can choose an international health track. In addition, the International Health Department of the School of Public Health runs several short-term training programs.

Boston University School of Public Health
715 Albany Street
Boston, MA 02118
tel.: 617-638-5299
email: sphadmis@bu.edu
website: http://www.bumc.bu.edu/ih

University of California/Berkeley, School of Public Health, offers programs leading to the M.A., M.Sc., M.P.H., Dr.P.H., and Ph.D. degrees.

University of California, Berkeley
School of Public Health
140 Warren Hall #7360
Berkeley, CA 94720-7360
tel.: 510-642-6531
website: http://www.sph.berkeley.edu

University of California/Los Angeles, School of Public Health offers programs leading to the M.P.H., Dr. P.H. M.Sc. and Ph.D. degrees. Students can specialize in a number of areas, including Biostatistics, Community Health Sciences, Environmental Health Sciences, Epidemiology, and Health Services.

UCLA School of Public Health
Box 951772
Los Angeles, CA 90095-1772
tel.: 310-825-5140
website: http://www.ph.ucla.edu

Case Western Reserve University offers programs leading to both the M.A. and Ph.D. degrees in Medical Anthropology with a concentration in International Health. Courses are offered in medical anthropological theory, epidemiology, international health research and policy, reproductive health, cross-cultural aging, primary health care, and nutritional anthropology. The university's Center for International Health provides a focal point for university activities in international health.

Dept. of Anthropology
Case Western Reserve University
10900 Euclid Ave.
Cleveland, OH 44106-7125
tel.: 216-368-2264.
website: http://www.cwru.edu/artsci/anth/anth.html

Columbia University's Division of Sociomedical Sciences offers an interdisciplinary doctoral program in Anthropology and Public Health.

Division of Sociomedical Sciences
Interdisciplinary Doctoral Program in Anthropology and Public
    Health
Columbia University
600 West 168th St.
New York, NY 10032
tel.: 212-305-5656
email: sms.sph@columbia.edu
website: http://www.cpmcnet.columbia.edu/dept/sph/smsl

Columbia University, Mailman School of Public Health offers numerous graduate degree programs in public health, including biostatistics, environmental health sciences, epidemiology, general public health, health policy and management, population and family health, and sociomedical sciences.

Mailman School of Public Health
Columbia University
535 West 116th St.

New York, NY 10023
tel.: 212-404-5893
website: http://www.cpmcnet.columbia.edu/dept/sph

Emory University, Rollins School of Public Health offers several Masters and Ph.D. programs, leading to the M.P.H., M.S.P.H. (Master of Science in Public Health), and Ph.D. degrees. Additionally it offers several dual degree programs.

Rollins School of Public Health
Emory University
1518 Clifton Road NE, First Floor
Atlanta, GA 30322
tel.: 404 -727-5481 or 404-727-3956
website: http://www.sph.emory.edu

George Washington University School of Public Health and Health Services offers numerous degrees and certificates in public health including the M.P.H. and M.H. (Masters of Health). Students can elect to concentrate in International Health Promotion or International Health Policy.

The George Washington University
School of Public Health
2300 I St., NW
Ross Hall 106
Washington, DC 20037
tel.: 202-994-3773
website: http://www.gwumc.edu/sphhs

Harvard University, School of Public Health offers four degree programs in public health – the Master of Science, Master of Public Health, Doctor of Science, and Doctor of Public Health -- in several departments including Health and Social Behavior, Health Policy and Management, and Population and International Health.

Harvard School of Public Health
677 Huntington Ave.
Boston, MA 02115
tel.: 617-432-1031
email: admisofc@hsph.harvard.edu
website: http://www.hsph.harvard.edu/Academics/pih/index.html

Johns Hopkins University, Bloomberg School of Public Health, offers programs leading to the MPH (Master of Public Health) as well as numerous joint degree and continuing education programs.

Bloomberg School of Public Health
Johns Hopkins University

615 North Wolfe St.
Baltimore, MD 21205
tel.: 410-955-5000
website: http://www.jhuccplorg

The University of Maryland offers a program leading to the degree of Master of Applied Anthropology (M.A.A) that includes a "Community, Health, and Development" specialty.
Department of Anthropology
University of Maryland
1111 Woods Hall
College Park, MD 20742-7415
tel.: 301-405-1423
email: anthgrad@deans.umd.edu
website: http://www.bsos.umd.edu/anth

The University of Michigan School of Public Health offers programs in biostatistics, environmental health sciences, epidemiology, health behavior and health education, and health management and policy, plus several interdepartmental concentrations, leading to the M.P.H., M.H.S.A. (Master of Health Services Administration), M.Sc., Ph.D., and Dr.P.H. degrees.
Office of Academic Affairs
School of Public Health
University of Michigan
109 Observatory St., 3537 SPH 1
Ann Arbor, MI 48109-2029
tel.: 734-764-5425
website: http://www.sph.umich.edu

Michigan State University offers M.A. and Ph.D. programs in Anthropology with a focus on International Health.
Department of Anthropology
Michigan State University
354 Baker Hall
East Lansing, MI 48824-1118
tel.: 517-353-2950
email: anthropology@ssc.msu.edu
website: http://www.ssc.msu.edu/anp

The University of Minnesota School of Public Health offers several advanced degrees, including the M.P.H., M.Sc., and Ph.D., through its divisions of Biostatistics, Environmental and Occupational Health, Epidemiology, and Health Services Research and Policy.

School of Public Health
University of Minnesota
Mayo Mail Code 197
420 Delaware St., SE
Minneapolis, MN 55455
tel.: 612-624-6669
website: http://www.sph.umn.edu

The University of North Carolina School of Public Health, which incorporates numerous public health centers, institutes and programs including an Office of Global Health, grants several health-related advanced degrees, including the M.H.A. (Master of Health Administration). The M.H.A. program offers courses in international public health.

University of North Carolina School of Public Health
Rosenau Hall, CB #7400
Chapel Hill, NC 27599-7400
tel.: 919-966-7676
website: http://www.sph.unc.edu

Oregon State University offers an M.A. program in Anthropology with a specialization in Health and Culture.

Department of Anthropology
Oregon State University
238 Waldo Hall
Corvallis, OR97331-6403
tel.: 541-737-4515
email: jyoung@orst.edu

The University of Pittsburgh Graduate School of Public Health grants the M.Sc., Ph.D., M.P.H., and Dr. P.H. degrees in seven academic departments. Students particularly interested in international health may elect to participate in a "Global Health Network Supercourse" for pre-health-professional students around the world, entitled "Epidemiology, the Internet, and Global Health."

Office of Student Affairs
114 Parran Hall
Graduate School of Public Health
University of Pittsburgh
Pittsburgh, PA 15261
tel.: 412-624-3002
website: http://www.pitt.edu/~gsphhome

St. Louis University, a Jesuit institution, grants the M.P.H., M.H.A. (Master of Health Administration), and Ph.D. degrees. The M.H.A. program, in particular, trains students to assume management positions in health services organizations "throughout the world."

St. Louis University
3545 Lafayette Ave.
St. Louis, MO 63104
tel. 1-800-782-6769
email: sphinfo@slu.edu
website: http://www.slu.edu/colleges/sph/slusph/

The University of South Florida offers a dual M.A. program in anthropology and public health.

Department of Anthropology
University of South Florida
4202 E. Fowler Ave.,
Tampa, FL 33620
tel.: 813-974-2011
website: http://www.cas.usf.edu/anthropology/grad

The University of Texas/Houston School of Public Health grants the M.P.H, Dr.P.H., M.Sc. and Ph.D. degrees in public health. A "module" in International and Family Health is offered.

UTHSC at Houston School of Public Health
P.O. Box 20186
Houston, TX 77225
tel.: 713-500-9000
website: utsph.sph.uth.tmc.edu

Tulane University School of Public Health and Tropical Medicine, which incorporates a Department of International Health and

Development, offers five Masters programs and two Doctoral programs in international health.

Tulane University School of Public Health and Tropical Medicine
1440 Canal St., Suite 2460
New Orleans, LA 70112
tel.: 1-800-676-5389
website: http://www.tulane.edu/~inhl/inhl.htm

Yale University School of Medicine incorporates an Epidemiology and Public Health Program that grants the M.P.H., M.Sc., and Ph.D. degrees in public health. M.P.H. students can specialize in any of six academic divisions, one of which is Global Health.

Department of Epidemiology and Public Health
Yale University
60 College St., PO Box 208034
New Haven, CT 06520-8034
tel.: 203-785-2844
website: info.med.yale.edu/eph/international.html

ORGANIZATIONS

Canadian Society for International Health
1 Nicholas Street, Suite 1105
Ottawa, Ontario, Canada K1N 7B7
tel.: 613-241-5785
email: csih@csih.org
website: http://www.csih.org

Center for Development and Population Activities (CEDPA)
1400 16th Street, NW, Suite 100
Washington, DC 20036
tel.: 202-667-1142
website: http://www.cedpa.org

Center for International Health and Cooperation
850 Fifth Ave.
New York, NY 10021
tel.: 212-434-2994
email: mail@cihc.org
website: http://www.cihc.org

Center for International Health Information (operates the USAID Health Information System)
1601 N. Kent Street, Suite 1001

Arlington, VA 22209
tel.: 703-524-5225
website: http://www.tfgi.com/cihi.asp

Centers for Disease Control and Prevention
1600 Clifton Road
Atlanta, GA 30333
tel.: 404-639-3311 or 1-800-311-3435
website: http://www.cdc.gov

Christian Connections for International Health (CCIH)
P.O. Box 291
Carrboro, NC 27510
tel.: 919-929-0650
email: ConnieGates@Ecunet.org
website: http://www.ccih.org

Earthwatch World Health Program
Earthwatch Institute
680 Mount Auburn St
P.O. Box 403
Watertown, MA 02272-9924
tel.: 1-800-776-0188
website: http://www.earthwatch.org

Family Health International (FHI)
P.O. Box 13950
Research Triangle Park, NC 27709
tel.: 919-544-7040
website: www.fhi.org

The Global Alliance for Women's Health
823 UN Plaza, Suite 712
New York, NY 10017
tel.: 212-286-0424
email: gawh@igc.apc.org
website: http://www.igc.org/beijing/ngo/gawh

The Global Forum
c/o World Health Organization
20 Avenue Appia
1211 Geneva 27, Switzerland
email: info@globalforumhealth.org
website: http://www.globalforumhealth.org

The Global Health Council (the major U.S. advocacy and networking
    organization for the international health field)
    1701 K Street, NW
    Washington, DC, 20006
    tel.: 202-833-5900
    email: ghc@globalhealth.org
    website: http://www.globalhealth.org

International Council of AIDS Service Organizations
    399 Church St., 4th Floor
    Toronto, Ontario M5B 2J6, Canada
    tel.: 1-416-340-2437
    website: http://www.icaso.org

International Women's Health Coalition
    24 East 21st St.
    New York, NY 10010
    tel.: 212-979-8500
    email: info@iwhc.org
    website: www.iwhc.org

Management Sciences for Health (a private, non-profit organization)
    165 Allandale Road
    Boston, MA 02130
    tel.: 617-524-7799
    email: development@msh.org
    website: http://www.msh.org

Pan American Health Organization (PAHO) (regional office of WHO)
    525 23rd Street, NW
    Washington, DC 20037
    tel.: 202-974-3000
    website: http://www.paho.org

The Population Council
    One Dag Hammarskjold Plaza
    New York, NY 10017
    tel.: 877-339-0500
    email: pubinfo@popcouncil.org
    website: http://www.popcouncil.org

UNAIDS
    20, Avenue Appia
    CH-1211 Geneva 27, Switzerland
    tel.: 4122-791-3666

email: unaids@unaids.org
website: http://www.unaids.org

World Federation of Public Health Associations
    c/o American Public Health Association
    800 I Street
    Washington, DC 20001-3710
    tel.: 202-777-2486
    email: allen.jones@apha.org
    website: http://www.apha.org/wfpha

World Health Organization (WHO)
    Avenue Appia 20
    1211 Geneva 27, Switzerland
    tel.: 41-22-791-2121
    website: http://www.who.org

INFORMATIONAL WEBSITES

American Medical Student Association Online (site contains list of
    international health opportunities)
    http://www.amsa.org/tf/inthlth

Association of Schools of Public Health
    http://www.asph.org

Catholic Medical Mission Board Online
    http://www.cmmb.org

Center for International Health Information
    http://www.tfgi.com/cihi.asp

FGM Research Home Page
    http://www.fgmnetwork.org

The George Washington Center for International Health
    http://www.gwu.edu/~cih

Global Health Disaster Network
    http://www.pitt.edu/~ghdnet/GHDNet

The Global Health Network
    http://www.pitt.edu/HOME/GHNet/GHNet.html

International Health Resource Informatics System
http://www.dante.med.utoronto.ca/ihris,htm

Student University Network for Social and International Health
http://www.icarus.med.utoronto.ca/sunsih.htm

13. APPLIED ENVIRONMENTAL ANTHROPOLOGY

SUGGESTED READINGS

Biersack, Aletta
1999. "Introduction: From the 'New Ecology' to the New Ecologies." American Anthropologist 101(1):5-18.

Bennett, John W.
1993. Human Ecology as Human Behavior: Essays in Environmental and Development Anthropology. New Brunswick, NJ: Transaction Publishers.

Bradford, Bonnie, and Margaret A. Gwynne
1995. Down to Earth: Community Perspectives on Health, Development, and the Environment. West Hartford, CT: Kumarian Press.

Bullard, Robert D.
1993. Confronting Environmental Racism. Boston: South End Press.

Chambers, Erve
2000. Native Tours: The Anthropology of Travel and Tourism. Prospect Heights, IL: Waveland Press.

Chew, Sing G.
2001. World Ecological Degradation. Walnut Creek, CA: AltaMira Press.

Crumley, Carole L.
2001. New Directions in Anthropology and Environment. Walnut Creek, CA: AltaMira Press.

Erocal, Denizhan (ed.)
1991. Environmental Management in Developing Countries. Paris: Organization for Economic Cooperation and Development.

Hirsch, Eric, and Michael O'Hanlon (eds.)
1995. The Anthropology of Landscape. Oxford: Clarendon.

Khan, Shahrukh Rafi
2002. Trade and Environment. London: Zed Books.

Khor, Martin, and Lim Li Lin (eds.)
2001. Economic, Environmental and Sustainable Livelihood
Initiatives (Vol. 1, Good Practices and Innovative Experiences in
the South). London: Zed Books.

Kottak, Conrad P.
1999. "The New Ecological Anthropology." American
Anthropologist 101(1):23-23-35.

Krech, Shepard III
1999. The Ecological Indian: Myth and History. New York: W.W.
Norton and Co.

Liebow, Edward
1995. "Inside the Decision-Making Process: Ethnography and
Environmental Risk Management." In Cerroni-Long, E.L.: Insider
Anthropology (NAPA Bulletin No. 17). Washington, DC: National
Association for the Practice of Anthropology.

McLaren, Deborah
1997. Rethinking Tourism and Ecotravel: The Paving of Paradise
and What You Can Do to Stop It. West Hartford, CT: Kumarian
Press.

Milton, Kay (ed.)
1993. Environmentalism: The View from Anthropology. London:
Routledge.

Milton, Kay
1996. Environmentalism and Cultural Theory: Exploring the Role
of Anthropology in Environmental Discourse. London: Routledge.

Molnar, Stephen, and Iva M. Molnar
2000. Environmental Change and Human Survival: Some
Dimensions of Human Ecology. Englewood Cliffs, NJ: Prentice
Hall.

Moran, Emilio F.
2000. Human Adaptability: An Introduction to Ecological
Anthropology. Boulder, CO: Westview Press.

Morse, Stephen, and Michael Stocking (eds.)
1995. People and Environment. London: UCL Press Limited.

Puntenney, P.J.

1995. Global Ecosystems: Creating Options through Anthropological Perspectives (NAPA Bulletin No. 15). Washington, DC: National Association for the Practice of Anthropology.

2000. "The Business of a Sustainable Career: Environmental Anthropology." In Sabloff, Paula L.W. (ed.): Careers in Anthropology: Profiles of Practitioner Anthropologists (NAPA Bulletin no. 20), pp. 34-38. Washington, DC: American Anthropological Association.

Roncoli, Carla (ed.)
2000. Anthropology and Climate Change: Challenges and Contributions (special issue). Practicing Anthropology 22(4).

Sivaramakrishnan, K.
1999. Modern Forests: Statemaking and Environmental Change in Colonial Eastern India. Stanford, CA: Stanford University Press.

Stevens, Stan (ed.)
1997. Conservation Through Cultural Survival: Indigenous Peoples and Protected Areas. Washington, DC: Island Press.

Tellegen, E., and Wolsink, M.
1998. Society and Its Environment: An Introduction. Amsterdam: Gordon and Breach.

Townsend, Patricia K.
2000. Environmental Anthropology: From Pigs to Policies. Prospect Heights, IL: Waveland Press.

World Bank
1992. Development and the Environment (World Development Report 1992). New York: Oxford University Press.

Zerner, Charles (ed.)
2000. People, Plants, and Justice: The Politics of Nature Conservation. New York: Columbia University Press.

JOURNALS

Conservation Biology
    Blackwell Science, Inc.
    350 Main St.
    Malden, MA 02148-5018
    tel.: 1-888-661-5800
    email: journals@blacksci.com
    website: http://www.jstor.org/journals

Environmental Conservation
    Cambridge University Press
    40 West 20th St.
    New York, NY 10011-4211
    tel.: 212-924-3239
    email: information@cup.org
    website: http://www.titles.cambrige.org/journals

Human Environments (online newsletter of the Environmental
    Anthropology Topical Intererst Group of the SfAA)
    website: http:ces.iisc.ernet.in/hpg/envis/doc9/jourhuman99410

National Geographic
    National Geographic Society
    1145 17th St., NW
    Washington, DC 20036-4688
    tel.: 1-800-647-546
    http://www.nationalgeographic.com

The New Environmentalist (online journal)
    http://www.thenewenvironmentalist.com

GRADUATE PROGRAMS

Boston University offers a program leading to the M.A. in Applied
Anthropology, designed for non-anthropologists either currently involved
or potentially interested in a number of applied fields, including
environmental management.
    Department of Anthropology
    Boston University
    232 Bay State Road
    Boston, MA 02215
    tel.: 617-353-2195
    email: oneil@bu.edu
    website: http://www.bu.edu/anthrop

The Catholic University of America offers M.A. and Ph.D. programs in ecological anthropology.

> Department of Anthropology
> The catholic University of America
> Washington, DC 20064
> tel.: 202-319-5080
> email: cua-anthro@cua.edu
> website: http://www.art-sciences.cua.edu/anth/grads.cfm

Cornell University offers a graduate minor in Conservation and Sustainable Development. Students must additionally seek a degree in a major field.

> Center for the Environment
> Education Program Coordinator
> 201 Rice Hall
> Ithaca, NY 14853-5601
> tel.: 607-255-7535
> email: cucfe@cornell.edu
> website: http://cfe.cornell.edu

The University of Georgia offers a Ph.D. program in Anthropology that includes a specialty in Ecological and Environmental Anthropology.

> Department of Anthropology
> University of Georgia
> 250 Baldwin Hall
> Athens, GA 30602-1619
> tel.: 706-542-3962
> email: anthro@arches.uga.edu
> website: anthro.dac.uga.edu

The University of Hawaii, Manoa, Department of Anthropology, offers a graduate program in Ecological Anthropology leading to the M.A. or Ph.D. degrees, with a focus on Southeast Asia and the Pacific.

> Department of Anthropology
> University of Hawaii at Manoa
> 2424 Maile Way
> Honolulu, Hawaii 96822
> email: anthprog@hawaii.edu
> website: http://www2.soc.hawaii.edu/css/anth/

Oregon State University offers a program leading to an M.A. in Applied Anthropology in which one area of specialization is natural resources and communities.

> Department of Anthropology
> Oregon State University

238 Waldo Hall
Corvallis, OR 97331-6403
tel.: 541-737-4515
email: jyoung@orst.edu

The University of Sussex (U.K.) offers a Masters program in Environment, Development, and Policy, through its Graduate Research Centre for Culture, Development, and Environment (CDE).
Dr. Richard Wilson
Centre for Culture, Development, and Environment
University of Sussex
Falmer, Brighton, BNI 9SJ, United Kingdom
tel.: (44) 01273 678722
email: R.Wilson@sussex.ac.uk

ORGANIZATIONS

Center for Biological Diversity
P.O. Box 710
Tucson, AZ 85702-0710
tel.: 520-623-5252
website: http://www.sw-center.org

Environmental Anthropology Topical Interest Group
American Anthropological Association
1703 New Hampshire Ave., NW
Washington, DC 20009
tel.: 703-528-1902
website: http://www.aaanet.org

Global Resource Action Center for the Environment (GRACE)
215 Lexington Ave., Suite 1001
New York, NY 10016
tel.: 212-726-9161
website: http://www.gracelinks.org

Earth Island Institute
300 Broadway, Suite 28
San Francisco, CA 94133
tel.: 415-788-3666
website: http://www.earthisland.org

Earthwatch Expeditions, Inc.
680 Mount Auburn St.,

P.O. Box 9104
Watertown, MA 02272
tel.: 1-800-461-0081
email: info@earthwatch.org
website: earthwatch.org

Friends of the Earth International
Box 19199
1000 GD
Amsterdam, The Netherlands
tel.: 31-20-622-1369
email: foei@foei.org
website: http://www.foei.org

Greenpeace U.S.
702 H Street NW, Suite 300
Washington DC 20001
tel: 1-800-326-0959
website: http://www.greenpeaceusa.org

Greenpeace International
Keizersgracht 176
1016 DW Amsterdam,
The Netherlands
email: supporter.services@ams.greenpeaceorg
website: http://www.greenpeace.org

The International Ecotourism Society
P.O. Box 688
Burlington, VT 05402
tel.: 802-651-9898
email: ecomail@ecotourism.org
website: http://www.ecotourism.org

Indigenous Environmental Network
P.O. Box 485
Bemidji, Minnesota 56619
tel.: 1-218-751-4967
website: http://www.ienearth.org

National Geographic Society
1145 17th St., NW
Washington, DC 20036-4688
tel.: 1-800-647-546
website: http://www.nationalgeographic.com

National Park Service
    1849 C Street, NW
    Washington DC 20240
    tel.: 202-208-6843
    website: http://www.nps.gov

National Wildlife Federation
    11100 Wildlife Center Drive
    Reston, VA 20190-5362
    tel.: 1-800-822-9919
    website: http://www.nwf.org

Rainforest Action Network
    221 Pine St., Suite 500
    San Francisco, CA 94104
    tel.: 415-398-4404
    email: rainforest@ran.org
    website: http://www.ran.org

United States Environmental Protection Agency
    401 M Street, SW
    Washington, DC 20460
    website: http://www.epa.gov

Sierra Club
    85 Second St., Second Floor
    San Francisco, CA 94105-3441
    tel.: 415-977-5500
    website: http://www.sierraclub.org

United Nations Environment Programme (UNEP)
    United Nations Avenue, Gigiri
    P.O. Box 30552
    Nairobi, Kenya
    tel.: 254-2-621234
    email: eisinfo@unep.org
    website: http://www.unep.org/

World Resources Institute
    1709 New York Ave., NW, Suite 700
    Washington, DC 20006
    tel.: 202-638-6300
    email: information@sierraclub.org
    website: http://www.wri.org/wri

World Wildlife Fund
1250 24th Street, NW
Washington, DC 20037
tel.: 202-293-4800
http://www.worldwildlife.org

INFORMATIONAL WEBSITES

Anthropology and Environment Section, AAA
http://www.dizzy.library.arizona.edu/ej/jpe/anthenv

The EcoJustice Network
http://www.igc.apc.org/envjustice

Environment and Society Internet Resource Guide
http://www.rpi.edu/dept/environ/guide

Environmental Anthropology Topical Interest Group of the SfAA
http://www.policycenter.com/policycenter/CAEP/caeppage.htm

Native Americans and the Environment
http://www.conbio.rice.edu/nae

Wildlife Conservation Society
http://www.wcs.org

U.S. National Park Service
http://www.nps.gov/

14. APPROPRIATE TECHNOLOGY AND TECHNOLOGY TRANSFER

SUGGESTED READINGS

Carr, M. (ed.)
1985. The AT Reader. London: Intermediate Technology Publications.

Douthwaite, Boru
2001. Enabling Innovation: A Practical Guide to Understanding and Fostering Technological Change. London: Zed Books.

Dudley, Eric
1993. The Critical Villager: Beyond Community Participation. London: Routledge.

Evans, Donald D., and Laurie Nogg Adler (eds.)
1982. Appropriate Technology for Development: A Discussion and Case Histories. Boulder, CO: Westview Press.

Fox, Robert (ed.)
1998. Technological Change: Methods and Themes in the History of Technology. Durham, UK: Harwood Academic Press.

Hazeltine, Barrett
2002. Field Guide of Appropriate Technology. San Diego: Academic Press.

Hazeltine, Barrett, Christopher Bull, and Lars Wanhammar
1999. Appropriate Technology: Tools, Choices, and Implications. San Diego: Academic Press.

Hornborg, Alf
2001. The Power of the Machine: Global Inequalities of Economy, Technology, and the Environment. Walnut Creek, CA: AltaMira Press.

International Federation for Women in Agriculture
1997. Environmentally Sound Technologies for Women in Agriculture. New Delhi: International Federation for Women in Agriculture.

James, Valentine (ed.)
1991. Urban and Rural Development in Third World Countries:

Problems of Populations in Developing Nations. Jefferson, NC: McFarland and Co., Inc., Publishers.

Kaplinsky, Raphael
1991. The Economies of Small: Appropriate Technology in a Changing World. London: Intermediate Technology Publications.

Kyambalesa, Henry
2001 The Quest for Technological Development. Lanham, MD: University Press of America.

Khor, Martin, and Lim Li Lin (eds.)
2002. Good Practices and Innovative Experiences in the South: Social Policies, Indigenous Knowledge, and Appropriate Technology. London: Zed Books.

Levitsky, J. (ed.)
1989. Microenterprises in Developing Countries. London: Intermediate Technology Publications.

Ngwainmbi, Emmanuel K.
1999. Exporting Communication Technology to Developing Countries: Sociocultural, Economic, and Educational Factors. Lanham, MD: University Press of America.

Stevens, Robert W. (ed.)
1991. Appropriate Technology: A Focus for the Nineties. London: Intermediate Technology Development Group.

Wilk, Richard
1996. "Sustainable Development: Practical, Ethical, and Social Issues in Technology Transfer." In Ishizuka, Kozo, et al.: Proceedings of the UNESCO-University of Tsukuba International Seminar on Traditional Technology for Environmental Conservation and Sustainable Development in the Asian Pacific Region, pp. 206-218. Tokyo, Japan: University of Tsukuba.

Willoughby, K.W.
1990. Technology Choice: A Critique of the Appropriate Technology Movement. London: Intermediate Technology Publications.

JOURNALS

Appropriate Technology (published 1991-2000)

United Nations Economic Commission for Western Asia
P.O. Box 11-8575
Beirut, Lebanon
website: http://www.escwa.org.lb/information/publications/main

Small Enterprise Development
Intermediate Technology Development Group
Schumacher Centre for Technology and Development
Bourton Hall
Bourton-on-Dunsmore
Rugby, Warks., CV23 9QZ, UK
tel.: 01788 661100
email: itdg@itdg.org.uk
website: www.itdg.org

GRADUATE PROGRAMS

The University of Arizona offers an M.A. program in Anthropology with
a specialization in Applied Anthropology, one focus of which is Culture,
Science, and Technology.
Department of Anthropology
University of Arizona
P.O. Box 210030
Tucson, AZ 85721-0030
tel.: 520-621-2585
website: w3.arizona.edu/anthro/
website for catalog: grad.admin.arizona.edu/catalog/catalog.htm

Colorado State University, which houses the Colorado State University
Appropriate Technology Institute (ATI) in its Department of Civil
Engineering, offers graduate degree programs in numerous areas,
including an M.A. in Anthropology.
Department of Anthropology
Colorado State University
Ft. Collins, CO 80523-1787
tel.: 970-491-5421
website: www.colostate.edu/Orgs/ATI

Cornell University offers a graduate minor in Conservation and
Sustainable Development. Students must additionally seek a degree in a
major field.
Center for the Environment
Education Program Coordinator
201 Rice Hall
Ithaca, NY 14853-5601

tel.: 607-255-7535
email: cucfe@cornell.edu
website: http://cfe.cornell.edu

Humboldt State University, which offers M.A. and M.Sc. degree programs, incorporates a Campus Center for Appropriate Technology (CCAT).
Campus Center for Appropriate Technology
Humboldt State University
Arcata, CA 95521
tel.: 707-826-3551
website: http://www.sorrel.humboldt.edu/~ccat

ORGANIZATIONS

Institute for Appropriate Technology
  89 Schoolhouse Road
  Summertown, TN 38483-0090
  tel.: 931-964-4474
  email: info@i4at.org
  website: http://www.i4at.org

Intermediate Technology Development Group
  Schumacher Centre for Technology and Development
  Bourton Hall
  Bourton-on-Dunsmore
  Rugby, Warks., CV23 9QZ, UK
  tel.: 01788 661100
  email: itdg@itdg.org.uk
  website: www.itdg.org

National Center for Appropriate Technology (NCAT)
  P.O. Box 2828
  Butte, MT 59702
  tel.: 406-494-4572 or 1-800-ask-NCAT
  website: www.ncat.org

Oxfam
  OXFAM House
  274 Banbury Road
  Oxford, OX 2 7DZ UK
  tel.: 44 (0) 1865 312610
  email: oxfam@oxfam.org.uk
  website: http://www.oxfam.org.uk

INFORMATIONAL WEBSITES

The Appropriate Technology Library Online Store
http://www.villageearth.org

Center for Renewable Energy and Sustainable Technology
http://www.solstice.crest.org

Communications for a Sustainable Future
http://www.csf.colorado.edu

Development Center for Appropriate Technology
http://www.cyberbites.com/dcat

International Institute for Sustainable Development (IISD)
http://www.iisd.ca

Technology Transfer
http://www.ids.ac.uk

15. MUSEUM WORK

SUGGESTED READINGS

Burcaw, G. Ellis
1997. Introduction to Museum Work. Walnut Creek, CA: AltaMira Press.

Dubin, Steven C.
1999. Displays of Power: Memory and Amnesia in the American Museum. New York: NYU Press.

Endicott, Kirk M., and Robert Welsch (eds.)
2001. "Do Museums Misrepresent Ethnic Communities Around the World?" In Kirk M. Endicott and Robert Welsch (eds.): Taking Sides: Clashing Views on Contemporary Issues in Anthropology, pp. 314-335. Guilford, CT: McGraw-Hill/Dushkin.

Haas, Jonathan
2000. "Anthropology in the Contemporary Museum." In Sabloff, Paula L.W. (ed.): Careers in Anthropology: Profiles of Practitioner Anthropologists (NAPA Bulletin no. 20), pp. 53-57. Washington, DC: American Anthropological Association.

Jackson, Jason Baird
2000. "Ethnography and Ethnographers in Museum-Community Partnerships." Practicing Anthropology 22(4):29-32.

Karp, Ivan, Christine Mullen Kreamer, and Steven D. Lavine
1992. Museums and Communities: The Politics of Public Culture. Washington, DC: Smithsonian Institution Press.

Kishenblatt-Gimblett, Barbara
1998. Destination Culture: Tourism, Museums, and Heritage. Los Angeles: University of California Press.

Krech, Shepard III, and Barbara A. Hail
1999. Collecting Native America, 1870-1960. Washington, DC: Smithsonian Institution Press.

Lord, Barry, and Gail Dexter Lord (eds.)
2000. Manual of Museum Planning (2nd ed.). Walnut Creek, CA: Altamira Press.

2001. The Manual of Museum Exhibitions. Walnut Creek, CA: Altamira Press.

Lubar, Steven, and Kathleen M. Kendrick
2001. Legacies: Collecting America's History at the Smithsonian. Washington, DC: Smithsonian Institution Press.

Stocking, George W. (ed.)
1988. Objects and Others: Essays on Museums and Material Culture. Madison, WI: University of Wisconsin Press.

Vandiver, Pamela B., et al. (eds.)
1992. Materials Issues in Art and Archaeology, Vol. III. Pittsburg, PA: Materials Research Society.

Washburn, Wilcomb E.
1998. "Is There a Museum 'Profession'?" In Washburn, Wilcomb E., Against the Anthropological Grain, pp. 149-166. New Brunswick, NJ: Transaction Publishers.

West, W. Richard, et al.
2000. The Changing Presentation of the American Indian: Museums and Native Cultures. Washington, DC: Smithsonian Institution/University of Washington Press/National Museum of the American Indian.

JOURNALS

Museum Anthropology
Susan S. Bean, Editor
Council for Museum Anthropology (an AAA section)
Peabody and Essex Museum
East India Square
Salem, MA 01970
tel.: 508-745-6776
website: http://www.nmnh.si.edu/cma/ma.html#3

Museum International
http://www.blackwellpublishers.co.uk/journals/muse

Museum News
American Association of Museums
Dept. 4002
Washington, DC 20042-4002
website: http://www.aam-us.org/pubp2.htm

GRADUATE PROGRAMS

Note: a list of museum training opportunities for anthropology students, which includes undergraduate courses and certificate programs in addition to M.A. and Ph.D. programs, can be found at http://www.nmnh.si.edu/cma/surveyhtml.

Arizona State University grants the M.A. degree in Anthropology with a concentration in Museum Studies.
> Museum Studies Program
> Department of Anthropology
> Arizona State University
> Tempe, AZ 85287-2402
> tel.: 602-965-6213
> email: museum.studies@asu.edu
> website: http://www.asu.edu.clas/anthropology

Brown University offers a program leading to an M.A. in Anthropology-Museum Studies.
> Dept. of Anthropology
> Brown University
> Box 1921
> Providence, RI 02912
> tel.: 401-863-7588
> email: Shapard-Krech-III@brown.edu
> website:
http://www.brown.edu/Facilities/Haffenreffer/Academic.html

The University of California, Berkeley offers a Ph.D. program in Social Cultural Anthropology with specializations in a number of domains of application, including museum anthropology.
> Department of Anthropology
> 207 Kroeber Hall #3710
> Berkeley, CA, 94720
> tel.: 510-642-3406
> website: http://www.ls.berkeley.edu/dept/anth/phdsoccult.intro.html

California State University, Chico offers an M.A. program with an option in Museum Studies.
> California State University, Chico
> W. First and Normal Sts.
> Chico, CA 95929-0400
> tel.: 530-898-6192
> email: anth@csuchico.edu/anth
> website: http://www.csuchico.edu/anth

University of Colorado, Boulder grants the degree of Master of Basic Science, Museum, and Field Studies.
University of Colorado, Boulder
Campus Box 218
Boulder, CO 80309-0218
tel.: 303-492-5437
email: steve.lekson@colorado.edu
website: http://www.colorado.edu/cumuseum

Columbia University, in conjunction with the American Museum of Natural History, offers a program leading to the M.A. in Museum Anthropology.
Department of Anthropology
Columbia University
452 Schermerhorn Extension
1200 Amsterdam Ave.
New York, NY 10027
tel.: 212-854-4552
website: http://www.columbia.edu/cu/anthropology

The University of Denver offers an M.A. in Anthropology with a museum studies concentration.
Department of Anthropology
University of Denver
2130 S. Race St.
Denver, CO 80208-2406
tel.: 303-871-2406
email: ckreps@du.edu
website: http://www.du.edu/anthro

Florida State University offers an interdepartmental program leading to a certificate in Museum Studies. The Department of Anthropology is a participant in this program.
Department of Anthropology
Florida State University
Tallahassee, FL 32306
tel.: 850-644-2525
website: http://www.fsu.edu/

George Washington University grants both the M.A. in Museum Studies and the M.A. in Anthropology with a concentration in Museum Training.
Museum Studies Program
George Washington University
801 22nd St., NW #T-215

Washington, DC 20052
tel.: 202-994-7020
website: http://www.gwy.edu/~mstd

The University of Missouri, St. Louis offers a program leading to an M.A. in Museum Studies.
Department of Anthropology
University of Missouri-St. Louis
8001 Natural Bridge Road
St. Louis, MO 63121-4499
tel.: 314-516-6020
email: svareid@umslvma.umsl.edu

San Francisco State University offers an M.A. in Museum Studies.
Museum Studies Program
College of Humanities
San Francisco State University
1600 Holloway
San Francisco, CA 94132
tel.: 415-338-1612
email: ellisl@sfsu.edu
website: http://www.sfsu.edu/~museumst

Seton Hall University has an M.A. Program in Museum Professions.
M.A. Program in Museum Professions
Dept. of Art and Music
Seton Hall University
400 South Orange Ave.
South Orange, NJ 07079
tel.: 201-761-7966

Texas Tech University offers an M.A. in Museum Science.
Museum of Texas Tech University
Fourth St. and Indiana Ave.
Lubbock, TX 79409-3191
tel.: 806-742-2442
email: mxljl@ttacs.ttu.edu
website: http://www.ttu.edu/~museum/

Wake Forest University offers an M.A. in Anthropology with elective courses in museum studies.
Museum of Anthropology
P.O. Box 7267
Wake Forest University
Winston Salem, NC 27109
tel.: 910-759-5166

email: moa@wfu.edu
website: http://www.wfu.edu/MOA

The University of Washington grants an M.A. degree in Museology.
Museology Program
Burke Museum
Box 353010 University of Washington
Seattle, WA 98195
tel.: 206-543-9680

ORGANIZATIONS

Note: State museum associations and councils in the U.S. are listed at
http:www.aam-us.org/links/links08.htm

American Association of Museums
1575 I St., NW, Suite 400
Washington, DC 20005
tel.: 202-289-1818
website http://www.aam-us.org

American Museum of Natural History
Central Park West at 79th St.
New York, NY 10024-5192
tel.: 212-769-5100
website: http://www.amnh.org

Council for Museum Anthropology, American Anthropological Association
c/o Rebecca Dobkins
Department of Anthropology
Willamette University
900 State Street
Salem, OR 97301
tel.: 503-370-6639
email: rdobkins@willamette.edu
website: http://www.nmnh.si.edu/cma

Field Museum
1400 S. Lake Shore Drive
Chicago, IL 60605-2496
tel. 312-922-9410
website: http://www.fmnh.org

George Gustav Heye Center (New York facility of the National Museum
of the American Indian)

Alexander Hamilton U.S. Custom House
One Bowling Green
New York, NY 10024
tel. 212-514-3700
website: http://www.nmai.si.edu/heye

National Museum of the American Indian (Washington, D.C. facility scheduled to open in 2004)
Cultural Resources Center
4220 Silver Hill Road
Suitland, MD 20746
tel.: 301-238-6624
website: http://www.nmai.si.edu

INFORMATIONAL WEBSITES

The American Association of Museums Online Bookstore Catalog
http://www.aam-us.org/text/bookstore.htm

Anthropology Exhibits on the WWW
http://lucy.ukc.ac.uk/exhibits.html

Anthropology Museums and Online Exhibits
http://www.academicinfo.net/anthmuseums.html

Anthropology Museums on the Web (links to museums with primarily cultural collections and exhibits)
http://www.luna.cas.usf.edu/~curtis/antmus.html

Department of Anthropology, National Museum of Natural History, Smithsonian Institution
http://www.nmnh.si.edu/departments/anthro.html

Museum Marketplace Online
http://www.mmo.aam-us.org

Museums Related to Anthropology
http://www.wsu.edu:8080/~i9248809/museums

U.S. Museum Jobs Online
http://www.museum-employment.com

WWW Virtual Library: Museums
http://vlmp.museophile.com/contacts/html

16. APPLIED EDUCATIONAL ANTHROPOLOGY

SUGGESTED READINGS

Berlak, Ann, and Sekani Moyenda
2001. Taking it Personally: Racismin the Classroom from Kindergarten to College. Philadelphia: Temple University Press.

Bigler, Ellen
1999. American Conversations: Puerto Ricans, White Ethnics, and Multicultural Education. Philadelphia: Temple University Press.

Bingham, Charles
2001. Schools of Recognition: Identity Politics and Classroom Practices. Lanham, MD: Rowman and Littlefield.

Borman, Kathryn M., et al.
1998. Ethnic Diversity in Communities and Schools: Recognizing and Building on Strengths. Stamford, CT: Ablex Publishhing Corp.

Carspecken, P.F.
1996. Critical Ethnography in Educational Research: A Theoretical and Practical Guide. New York: Routledge.

Champagne, Duane, and Jay Stauss (eds.)
2001. Native American Studies in Higher Education: Models for Collaboration Between Universities and Indigenous Nations. Walnut Creek,k CA: AltaMira Press.

Chavez, Rudolfo, and James O'Donnell (eds.)
1998. Speaking the Unpleasant: The Politics of (Non) Engagement in the Multicultural Education Terrain. Albany: State University of New York Press.

Cohen, Mark Nathan
1998. Culture of Intolerance: Chauvinism, Class, and Racism in the United States. New Haven, CT: Yale University Press.

Cushner, Kenneth (ed.)
1998. International Perspectives on Intercultural Education. Mahwah, NJ: Lawrence Erlbaum Associates.

Davidson, Ann
1996. Making and Molding Identity in Schools: Student Narratives

on Race, Gender, and Academic Achievement. Albany: State
University of New York Press.

Fine, Michelle
1991. Framing Dropouts: Notes on the Politics of an Urban Public
High School. Albany: State University of New York Press.

1994 (ed.). Chartering Urban School Reform: Reflections on
Public High Schools in the Midst of Change. New York: Teachers
College Press.

Frank, Carolyn
1999. Ethnographic Eyes: A Teacher's Guide to Classroom
Observation. Portsmouth, NH: Heinemann.

Freeman, Rebecca D.
1998. Bilingual Education and Social Change. Philadelphia:
Multilingual Matters.

Gandara, Patricia
2000. The Dimensions of Time and the Challenge of School
Reform. Albany, NY: State University of New York Press.

Gorski, Paul C.
2001. Multicultural Education and the Internet: Intersections and
Integration. Boston: McGraw-Hill Higher Education.

Henze, Rosemary C., and Mary E. Hauster
1999. Personalizing Culture Through Anthropological and
Educational Perspectives. Santa Cruz, CA: Center for Research
on Education, Diversity, and Excellence, University of
California/Santa Cruz.

Hess, G. Alfred, Jr.
1995. Restructuring Urban Schools: A Chicago Perspective. New
York: Teachers College Press.

Hones, Donald F., and Cher Shou Cha
1999. Educating New Americans: Immigrant Lives and Learning.
Mahwah, NJ: Lawrence Erlbaum Associates.

Kingston-Mann, Esther, and Tim Sieber (eds.)
2001. Achieving Against the Odds: How Academics Become
Teachers of Diverse Students. Philadelphia: Temple University
Press.

Kozaitis, Kathryn A.
2000. "Anthropological Influence on Urban Educational Reform."
Practicing Anthropology 22(4):37-44.

Lancy, David F.
2001. Studying Children and Schools. Prospect Heights, IL:
Waveland Press.

Levinson, Bradley A.U., et al. (eds.)
2000. Schooling the Symbolic Animal Solcial and Cultural
Dimensions of Education. Blue Ridge Summit, PA: Rowman and
Littlefield Publishers, Inc.

Levinson, Bradley, D. Foley, and D. Holland (eds.)
1996. The Cultural Production of the Educated Person. Albany:
State University of New York Press.

Manning, Kathleen
2000. Rituals, Ceremonies, and Cultural Meaning in Higher
Education. Westport, CT: Bergin and Garvey.

McGinty, Sue
1999. Resilience, Gender, and Success at School. New York:
Peter Lang Publishing, Inc.

Nespor, Jan
1997. Tangled Up in School: Politics, Space, Bodies, and Signs in
the Educational Process. Mahwah, NJ: Lawrence Erlbaum
Associates.

Nieto, Sonia
1999. The Light in Their Eyes: Creating Multicultural Learning
Communities. New York: Teachers College Press.

Pang, Valerie O.
2001. Multicultural Education: A Caring-Centered, Reflective
Approach. New York: McGraw-Hill.

Rice, Patricia C., and David W. McCurdy (eds.)
2000. Strategies in Teaching Anthropology. Upper Saddle River,
NJ: Prentice Hall.

Solomon, R. Patrick
1992. Black Resistance in High School: Forging a Separatist
Culture. Albany: State University of New York Press.

Spindler, George (ed.)
1997. Education and Cultural Process: Anthropological
Approaches. Prospect Heights, IL: Waveland Press.

Spindler, George, and Louise Spindler
2000. Fifty Years of Anthropology and Education, 1950-2000: A
Spindler Anthology. Mahwah, NJ: Lawrence Erlbaum Associates.

Valverde, Leonard A., and Louis A. Castenell (eds.)
1998. The Multicultural Campus: Strategies for Transforming
Higher Education. Walnut Creek, CA: AltaMira Press.

Vermeulen, Hans, and Joel Perlman
2000. Immigrants, Schooling, and Social Mobility: Does Culture
Make a Difference? New York: Palgrave.

Wexler, Philip
1992. Becoming Somebody: Toward a Social Psychology of
School. London: Falmer Press.

JOURNALS

Anthropology and Education Quarterly
Council on Anthropology and Education (an AAA section)
Dr. Teresa McCarty, Editor
University of Arizona Dept. of Language, Reading, and Culture
1430 East 2nd St.
P.O. Box 210069
College of Education Bldg., Rm. 512
Tucson, AZ 85721-0069
tel.: 520-621-1311
email: aequart@email.arizona.edu
website: http://www.aaanet.org/cae/aeq

Linguistics and Education
Elsevier Science, Ltd.
P.O. Box 945
New York, NY 10159-0945
tel.: 212-633-3730 or 1-888-437-636
email: usinfo-f@elsevier.com
website: http://www.elsevier.com

GRADUATE PROGRAMS

Note: A comprehensive list of graduate programs in Anthropology and Education is available at http://www.aaanet.org/cae/guide_offerings.html

The University of California, Berkeley offers a Ph.D. program in Social Cultural Anthropology with specializations in a number of domains of application, including the anthropology of education.
Department of Anthropology
207 Kroeber Hall #3710
Berkeley, CA, 94720
tel.: 510-642-3406
website: http://www.ls.berkeley.edu/dept/anth/phdsoccult.intro.html

Teachers College, Columbia University offers programs leading to any of four degrees in Anthropology and Education: the M.A., M.Ed. (Master of Education), Ed.D. (Doctor of Education), or Ph.D.
Teachers College, Columbia University
Department of International and Transcultural Studies
Programs in Applied Anthropology and Anthropology and
Education
Box 19, 525 West 120th St.
New York, NY 10027
tel.: 212-678-3309
email: lc137@columbia.edu

George Mason University, Graduate School of Education, grants Master of Education (M.Ed.), M.A., and Ph.D. degrees in Education. Courses in Educational Anthropology are available.
Graduate School of Education
George Mason University
MSN 4B4
4400 University Drive
Fairfax, VA 22030-4444
tel.: 703-993-2010
email: gseadmit@gmu.edu
website: http://www.gse.gmu.edu/programs

The University of South Florida offers programs leading to both the M.A. and Ph.D. degrees in Applied Anthropology. One faculty specialization is educational anthropology.
Department of Anthropology
University of South Florida
4202 E. Fowler Ave.,
Tampa, FL 33620
tel.: 813-974-2011
website: http://www.cas.usf.edu/anthropology/grad

ORGANIZATIONS

American Indian Higher Education Consortium
P.O. Box 720
Mancos, CO 81328
tel.: 970-533-9170
website: http://www.aihec.org

Council on Anthropology and Education (CAE)
American Anthropological Association
4350 North Fairfax Drive, Suite 640
Arlington, VA 22203
tel. 703-528-1902
website: http://www.aaanet.org/cae

INFORMATIONAL WEBSITES

AEQ (Anthropology and Education Quarterly) Book Reviews Online
http://www.aaanet.org/cae/aeq/br/index.htm

Educational Anthropology: A Guide to Library Resources
http://library.adelaide.edu.au/guide/soc/anthro/subj/educ.html

17. APPLIED ARCHAEOLOGY
AND CULTURAL RESOURCES MANAGEMENT

SUGGESTED READINGS

Ashmore, Wendy, and A. Bernard Knapp (eds.)
1999. Archaeologies of Landscape. Malden, MA: Blackwell.

Banning, E.B.
(forthcoming). Archaeological Surveys. Norwell, MA: Kluwer
Plenum.

Ferguson, T.J.
2000. "Applied Anthropology in the Management of Native
American Cultural Resources: Archaeology, Ethnography, and
History of Traditional Cultural Places." In Sabloff, Paula L.W. (ed.):
Careers in Anthropology: Profiles of Practitioner Anthropologists
(NAPA Bulletin no. 20), pp. 15-17. Washington, DC: American
Anthropological Association.

Garrow, Patrick H.
1993. "Ethics and Contract Archaeology." Practicing Anthropology
15(3):10-13.

Goldberg, Paul, Vance T. Holliday and Reid Ferring (eds.)
2001. Earth Sciences and Archaeology. Norwell, MA: Kluwer
Plenum.

Hardesty, Donald L., Barbara J. Little, and Don Fowler
2000. Assessing Site Significance: A Guide for Archaeologists
and
Historians. Walnut Creek, CA: AltaMira Press.

Hodder, Ian
2001. Archaeological Theory Today. Malden, MA: Blackwell.

Hodder, Ian, and Rolbert Preucel (eds.)
1996. Contemporary Archaeology in Theory. Malden, MA:
Blackwell.

Johnson, Matthew
1999. Archaeological Theory: An Introduction. Malden, MA:
Blackwell.

Kerber, Jordan E. (ed.)
    1994. Cultural Resource Management: Archaeological Research,
    Preservation Planning, and Public Education in the
    Northeastern US. Westport, CT: Bergin and Garvey.

King, Thomas F.
    1998. Cultural Resource Laws and Practice: An Introductory
    Guide. Walnut Creek, CA: AltaMira Press.

    2000. Federal Planning and Historic Places. Walnut Creek, CA:
    AltaMira Press.

    2002. Rethinking Cultural Resources Management. Walnut Creek,
    CA: AltaMira Press.

McManamon, Francis P.
    2000. "A Public Archaeologist in a Public Agency." In Sabloff,
    Paula L.W. (ed.): Careers in Anthropology: Profiles of Practitioner
    Anthropologists (NAPA Bulletin no. 20), pp. 58-63. Washington,
    DC: American Anthropological Association.

Neumann, Thomas W., and Robert M. Sanford
    2001a. Cultural Resources Archaeology: An Introduction. Walnut
    Creek, CA: AltaMira Press.

    2001b. Practicing Archaeology: A Training Manual for Cultural
    Resources Archaeology. Walnut Creek, CA: AltaMira Press.

Pastron, Allen G.
    1994 (orig. 1988). "Opportunities in Cultural Resources
    Management." In Podolefsky, Aaron, and Peter J. Brown (eds.):
    Applying Anthropology (3rd ed.). Mountain View, CA: Mayfield.

Praetzellis, Adrian
    2000. Death by Theory: A Tale of Mystery and Archaeological
    Theory. Walnut Creek, CA: AltaMira Press.

Stapp, Darby (ed.)
    1998. Changing Paradigms in Cultural Resource Management.
    Practicing Anthropology 20(3):1-33 (special issue).

Vitelli, Karen D. (ed.)
    1996. Archaeological Ethics. Walnut Creek, CA: AltaMira Press.

Washburn, Wilcomb E.

1998. "Do Ideology and Archaeology Mix?" In Wilcomb E. Washburn: <u>Against the Anthropological Grain</u>, pp. 109-112. New Brunswick, NJ: Transaction Publishers.

Williamson, Ray A., and Paul R. Nickens (eds.)
2000. <u>Science and Technology in Historic Preservation</u>. Norwell, MA: Kluwer Plenum.

JOURNALS

<u>American Antiquity</u>
Society for American Archaeology
Tim Kohler, Editor
Washington State University
Department of anthro9pology
Pullman, WA 99164-2770
tel.: 509-335-2770
email: aaq@wsu.edu
website: http://www.saa.org/Publications/AmAntiq/amantiq.html

<u>Archaeology</u>
36-36 33rd St.
Long Island City, NY 11106
tel.: 718-472-3050
website: http://www.archeologyl.org/magazine

<u>Archaeology and Public Education</u> (a newsletter)
Society for American Archaeology
Dr. Ed Friedman
Bureau of Reclamation
P.O. Box 25007, D5300,
Denver, CO, 80225.

<u>Journal of Archaeological Method and Theory</u>
Kluwer Plenum
101 Philip Drive
Norwell, MA 02061
tel.: 1-866-269-WKAP
website: http://www.wkap.nl

<u>Journal of Archaeological Science</u>
Elsevier Science, Ltd.
P.O. Box 945
New York, NY 10159-0945
tel.: 212-633-3730 or 1-888-437-636

email: usinfo-f@elsevier.com
website: http://www.elsevier.com

Journal of Field Archaeology
Boston University Scholarly Publications
985 Commonwealth Ave.
Boston, MA 02215
tel. 617-353-4106
website: http://jfa-www.bu.edu/Biz/jfa

Journal of Material Culture (available electronically)
website: http://www.sagepub.co.uk

Oxford Journal of Archaeology
Blackwell Publishing
350 Main St.
Malden, MA 02148
tel.: 781-388-8200
website: http://www.blackwellpublishers.co.uk/journals/OJOA

The SAA Archaeological Record (formerly SAA Bulletin)
c/o John Kantner, Editor
Dept. of Anthropology and Geography
Georgia State University
33 Gilmer St.
Atlanta, GA 30303-3083
tel.: 404-651-1761
email: kantner@gsu.edu
website: http://www.saa.org/Publications/thesaaarchrec

GRADUATE PROGRAMS

Note: Information on academic programs in archaeology is available on the Internet at http://www.saa.org/careers/academic.html. The programs listed below place special emphasis on applied archaeology and cultural resources management.

SUNY Buffalo offers degree programs leading to both the M.A. and Ph.D. degrees in Anthropology. Areas of specialization include archaeological survey.
Department of Anthropology
389 Millard Fillmore Academic Center
Buffalo, NY 14261-0005
tel.: 716-645-2414
email: mal@adsu.buffalo.edu

website: http://www.wings.buffalo.edu/anthropology

The University of California, Berkeley offers a Ph.D. program in Social Cultural Anthropology with specializations in a number of domains of application, including historical archaeology and material culture.
Department of Anthropology
207 Kroeber Hall #3710
Berkeley, CA, 94720
tel.: 510-642-3406
website: http://www.ls.berkeley.edu/dept/anth/phdsoccult.intro.html

Indiana University, Bloomington offers graduate degree programs leading to the M.A. or Ph.D. in Anthropology with a specialty in archaeology and a "Track in Archaeology and Social Context."
Department of Anthropology
Indiana University
Student Building 130
Bloomington, IN 47405
tel.: 812-855-1041
email: cadamus@indiana.edu
website: http://www.indiana.edu/~anthro

The **University of Kentucky** offers both Master's and Ph.D. degree programs with a specialty in archaeology that incorporates "a strong focus on applied research."
Department of Anthropology
University of Kentucky
Lexington, KY 40506
tel.: 606-257-2710
website: http://www.uky.edu/ArtsSciences/Anthropology

McGill University offers M.A. and Ph.D. degree programs with a concentration in anthropological archaeology.
Department of Anthropology
Room 717 Stephen Leacock Building
855 Sherbrooke St., West
Montreal Quebec, Canada H3A 2T7
tel.: 514-398-4300
website: http://www.arts.mcgill.ca/programs/anthro

The University of Memphis offers an M.A. degree in Anthropology with a focus on practicing anthropology in four areas, one of which is cultural resources management.
Department of Anthropology
The University of Memphis
Memphis, TN 38152

tel.: 901-878-2080
website: http://www.people.memphis.edu/~anthropology/
email: finerman@memphis.edu

Michigan State University offers a degree program leading to the Masters in the Professional Applications of Anthropology (MAPAA), which specifically prepares students for careers a practicing anthropologists in professional areas cultural resources management.
Department of Anthropology
Michigan State University
354 Baker Hall
East Lansing, MI 48824-1118
tel.: 517-353-2950
email: anthropology@ssc.msu.edu
website: http://www.ssc.msu.edu/anp

Oregon State University offers an M.A. in Applied Anthropology; special faculty interests include both historic archaeology and cultural resources management.
Department of Anthropology
Oregon State University
238 Waldo Hall
Corvallis, OR 97331-6403
tel.: 541-737-4515
email: jyoung@orst.edu

The University of South Florida offers programs leading to both the M.A. and Ph.D. degrees in Applied Anthropology (one faculty specialization is cultural resources management), and to the M.A. in Public Archaeology.
Department of Anthropology
University of South Florida
4202 E. Fowler Ave.,
Tampa, FL 33620
tel.: 813-974-2011
website: http://www.cas.usf.edu/anthropology/grad

The University of York offers degree programs leading to the degrees of MSc in Archaeological Information Systems, M.A. in Archaeological Research, and M.A. in Archaeological Heritage Management, among others.
Department of Archaeology
University of York
King's Manor
York Y01 7EP, U.K.
tel.: 01904 433936

email: pab11@york.ac.uk
website: http://www.york.ac.uk/depts/arch

ORGANIZATIONS

Advisory Council on Historic Preservation
 1100 Pennsylvania Ave., Suite 809
 Old Post Office Building
 Washington, DC 20004
 tel.: 202-606-8503
 website: http://www.achp.gov

Archaeological Conservancy
 5301 Central Ave., NE, Suite 1218
 Albuquerque, NM 87108-1517
 tel. 505–266-1540
 website: http://www.americanarchaeology.com/aaabout.html

Archaeological Institute of America
 Boston University
 656 Beacon St.
 Bston, MA 12215-2006
 tel.: 617-353-9361
 email: aia@aia.bu.edu
 website: http://archaeological.org

Archaeology Division, American Anthropological Association
 4350 North Fairfax Drive, Suite 640
 Arlington, VA 22203-1620
 tel.: 703-528-1902
 website: http://www.aaanet.org/ad/index/htm

Society for American Archaeology
 900 Second St., NE, #12
 Washington, DC 20002-3557
 tel.: 202-789-8200
 email: headquarters@saa.org
 website: http://www.saa.org

Society for Historical Archaeology
 PO Box 30446
 Tucson, AZ 85751-0446
 tel.: 520-886-8006
 email:" the_sha@mindspring.com
 website http://shaonline.org

INFORMATIONAL WEBSITES

About Archaeology
http://www.archaeology.about.com/science/archaeology/mbody/htm

Archaeology Film Reviews
http://www.anth.ucsb.edu/videos/index.html

Archaeology Online Archive
http://www.archaeology.org/magazine.php?page=online/archive

ArchNet (WWW Virtual Library – Archaeology)
http://archnet.asu.edu

Archaeological Conservancy
http://www.americanarchaeology.com/aaabout.html

International Cultural Property Protection
http://exchanges.staate.gov/culprop/

The World Heritage List
http://whc.unesco.org//heritage.htm

18. APPLIED PHYSICAL ANTHROPOLOGY AND FORENSICS

SUGGESTED READINGS

(n.a.)
> 1994 (orig. 1982). "Anthropometry, Assassinations, and Aircraft Disasters: A Career in Forensic Anthropology." In Podolefsky, Aaron, and Peter Brown (eds.): Applying Anthropology, pp. 69-71. Mountain View, CA: Mayfield.

Alexander, R. McNeill
> 2000. Bones: The Unity of Form and Function. Boulder, CO: Westview Press.

Bramblett, Claud A.
> 1994. Patterns of Primate Behavior (2nd ed.). Prospect Heights, IL: Waveland Press.

Burns, Karen Ramey
> 1999. The Forensic Anthropology Training Manual. Englewood Cliffs, NJ: Prentice Hall.

Camenson, Blythe
> 1998. Opportunities in Zoos and Aquariums. Lincolnwood, IL: VGM Career Horizons.

Ciochon, Russell L., and Richard Nisbett (eds.)
> 1998. The Primate Anthology: Essays on Primate Behavior, Ecology and Conservation from Natural History. Englewood Cliffs, NJ: Prentice Hall.

Evans, Colin
> 1996. The Casebook of Forensic Detection: How Science Solved 100 of the World's Most Baffling Crimes. New York: John Wiley and Sons.

Fairgrieve, Scott I. (ed.)
> 1999. Forensic Osteological Analysis: a Book of Case Studies. Springfield, IL: Charles C. Thomas Publisher

Gordon, Claire C. (ed.)
> 1993. Race, Ethnicty, and Applied Bioanthropology (NAPA Bulletin No. 13). Washington, DC: National Association for the Practice of Anthropology.

Haglund, William D.
    1993. "Beyond the Bare Bones: Recent Developments in Forensic
    Anthropology." Practicing Anthropology 15(3):17-19.

Katzenberg, M. Anne, and Shelley R. Saunders (eds.)
    2000. Biological Anthropology of the Human Skeleton. New York:
    John Wiley and Sons.

Nafte, Myriam
    2000. Flesh and Bone: An Introduction to Forensic Anthropology.
    Durham, NC: Carolina Academic Press.

Prag, John, and Richard Neave
    1997. Making Faces: Using Forensic and Archaeological
    Evidence. College Station, TX: Texas A&M University Press.

Rathbun, Ted A., and Jane E. Buikstra (eds.)
    1984. Human Identification: Case Studies in Forensic
    Anthropology. Springfield, IL: Charles C. Thomas.

Rhine, Stanley
    1998. Bone Voyage: A Journey in Forensic Anthropology.
    Albuquerque: Univ. of New Mexico Press.

JOURNALS

American Journal of Human Biology
    John Wiley and Sons
    605 Third Ave., 9th Fl.
    New York, NY 10158-0012
    website: http://www.wiley.com/cda/product/0,,B%7C4670.00

American Journal of Physical Anthropology
    John Wiley and Sons
    605 Third Ave., 9th Fl.
    New York, NY 10158-0012
    website: http://www.interscience.wiley.com/jpages/0002-9483

American Journal of Primatology
    John Wiley and Sons
    605 Third Ave., 9th Fl.
    New York, NY 10158-0012
    website: http://www.asp.org/ajp/

Journal of Forensic Sciences
6700 Woodlands Parkway, Suite 230-308
The Woodlands, TX 77381
tel.: 936-273-4270
email: jfs.editor@att.net
website: http://www.aafs.org/journal1.htm

Physical Anthropology (newsletter of the American Association of
Physical Anthropologists; available online only)
website: http://www.physanth.org/newsletter/physanthnews.html

Zoo Biology
John Wiley and Sons, Inc.
Attn: Journals Admin. Dept. UK
111 River St.
Hoboken, NJ 07030
tel.: 201-748-6645
website: http://www.interscience.wiley.com

GRADUATE PROGRAMS

Note: See the website of the American Association of Physical
Anthropologists, at http://www.physanth.org/gradprogs, for a list of
departmental graduate programs in physical anthropology. The programs
listed below are either very well known or offer training in an area of
applied physical anthropology, such as applied biological anthropology or
forensics.

Duke University, Department of Biological Anthropology and Anatomy,
offers a program leading to a Ph.D. in Biological Anthropology.
The Graduate School
127 Allen Building
Duke University
Durham, NC 27708
website: http:www.baa.duke.edu

The University of Florida graduate program in Biological Anthropology
includes a sub-specialty in skeletal biology in forensic and
paleoanthropological contexts.
Department of Anthropology
University of Florida
Gainesville, FL 32611
tel.: 352-392-2031
website: http://www.anthro.ufl.edu

The University of Illinois, Chicago, through its Department of Criminal Justice and College of Pharmacy, offers a program leading to the Master of Science in Forensic Science.
 University of Illinois at Chicago
 1007 West Harrison St., M/C 141
 Chicago, IL 60607
 tel.: 312-996-2383
 website: http://www.uic.edu

Indiana University offers graduate degree programs in Anthropology, at both the M.A. and Ph.D. levels, with a specialty in bioanthropology.
 Department of Anthropology
 Indiana University
 Student Building 130
 Bloomington, IN 47405
 tel.: 812-855-1041
 email: cadamus@indiana.edu
 website: http://www.indiana.edu/~anthro

The University of Maryland offers a program leading to the Master of Applied Anthropology (MAA) degree with an applied biological anthropology track.
 Department of Anthropology
 University of Maryland
 1111 Woods Hall
 College Park, MD 20742-7415
 tel.: 301-405-1423
 email: anthgrad@deans.umd.edu
 website: http://www.bsos.umd.edu/anth

The **State University of New York at Binghamton** offers a Ph.D. program with a specialty in biological anthropology.
 Director of Graduate Studies
 Department of Anthropology
 Binghamton University
 Binghamton, NY 13902-6000
 tel.: 607-777-2738
 email: pangolin@binghamton.edu

The **State University of New York at Stony Brook** houses the Interdepartmental Doctoral Program in Anthropological Sciences (IDPAS), which includes faculty from Anatomical Sciences. The IDPAS, currently the top-ranked Anthropology program in the U.S., grants the Ph.D. in Anthropological Sciences.
 Department of Anthropology
 SBS Building, 5th Floor

State University of New York at Stony Brook
Stony Brook, NY 11794-4364
tel.: 631-632-7620
website: http://www.sunysb.edu/anthro

Ohio State University, Department of Anthropology, grants the Ph.D. degree with a specialty in physical anthropology.
Department of Anthropology
Ohio State University
244 Lord Hall
124 West 17th Ave.
Columbus, OH 43210
tel.: 614-292-4149
website: http://www.monkey.ss.ohio-state.edu

ORGANIZATIONS

American Board of Forensic Anthropology
    Anthropology Dept.
    California State University, Chico
    W. First and Normal Sts.
    Chico, CA 95929-0400
    tel.: 530-898-6192
    website: http://www.csuchico.edu/anth/ABFA/#Background

American Academy of Forensic Sciences
    PO Box 669
    Colorado Springs, CO 80901-0669
    website: http://www.aafs.org/

American Association of Physical Anthropologists
    P.O. Box 1897
    Lawrence, KS 66044-8897
    email: pwalker@anth.ucsb.edu
    website: http://www.physanth.org

Biological Anthropology Section, American Anthropological Association
    4350 North Fairfax Drive, Suite 640
    Arlington, VA 22203-1620
    tel.: 703-528-1902
    website: http://www.aaanet.org/bas/index.htm

American Society of Primatologists
    c/o Steven J. Shapiro
    Dept. of Veterinary Sciences

UTMDACC
650 Cool Water Drive
Bastrop, TX 78602-6621
tel.: 512-321-3991
email: sschapir@mdanderson.org
website: http://www.asp.org

Canadian Association for Physical Anthropology
Dr. Charles Fitzgerald
Dept. of Anthropology
McMaster University
1280 Main St.
West Hamilton, Ontario, Canada ON L8S 4L9
email: fitzgerl@mcmaster.ca
website: http://citd.scar.utoronto.ca/CAPA

INFORMATIONAL WEBSITES

The Biological Anthropology Web
http://www.bioanth.org

C.A. Pound Human Identification Laboratory
http://web.anthro.ufl.edu/c.a.poundlab/poundlab/htm

Careers in Physical Anthropology
American Association of Physical Anthropologists
http://www.physanth.org/careers/

Dian Fossey Gorilla Fund
http://www.dianfossey.org

Federal Bureau of Investigation
http://www.fbi.gov

Human Biology Association
http://www.yorku.ca/hba

Jane Goodall Institute
http://www.janegoodall.org

Midori's Forensic Anthropology Page
http://people.uncw.edu/albertm

Midwest Bioarchaeology and Forensic Anthropology Association
(BARFAA)

http://www.luc.edu/depts/anthropology/BARFAA

Non-Academic Careers in Physical Anthropology
http://www.weber.ucsd.edu/~jmoore/bioanthro/brochure2.html

Orangutan Foundation International
http://www.orangutan.org/index1.htm

US Army Central Identification laboratory:
http://www.qmfound.com/Army_Central_Identification_Laboratory_
Hawaii.htm

Zeno's Forensic Site
http://forensic.to/forensic.html

19. APPLIED ANTHROPOLOGICAL LINGUISTICS

SUGGESTED READINGS

Bailey, Richard W.
  1991. Images of English: A Cultural History of the Language. Ann Arbor, MI: University of Michigan Press.

Blount, Ben
  1995. Language, Culture, and Society: A Book of Readings (2nd ed.). Prospect Heights, IL: Waveland Press.

Bonvillain, Nancy
  2000. Language, Culture, and Communication: The Meaning of Messages (3rd ed.). Englewood Cliffs, NJ: Prentice Hall.

Crawford, James
  1999. Bilingual Education: History, Politics, Theory, and Practice (4th ed.) Los Angeles: Bilihngual Educational Services.

Duranti, Alessandro (ed.)
  2001. Linguistic Anthropology: A Reader. Oxford: Blackwell.

Fishman, Joshua
  1999. Handbook of Language and Ethnic Identity. Oxford, UK: Oxford University Press.

Foley, William
  1997. Anthropological Linguistics. Malden, MA: Blackwell.

Hudson, Grover
  1999. Essential Introductory Linguistics. Malden, MA: Blackwell.

John-Steiner, Vera, Carolyn P. Panofsky, and Larry W. Smith (eds.)
  1994. Sociocultural Approaches to Language and Literacy: An Interactionist Perspective. New York: Cambridge University Press.

Kloss, H.
  1998. The American Bilingual Tradition. Washington, DC: Clearinghouse on Languages and Linguistics.

Krashen, Stephen
  1996. Under Attack: The Case Against Bilingual Education. Culver City, CA: Language Education Associates.

Salzmann, Zdenek
1998. Language, Culture, and Society: An Introduction to Linguistic Anthropology (2nd ed.). Boulder, CO: Westview Press.

Saville-Troike, Muriel
2001. The Ethnography of Communication. Malden, MA: Blackwell.

Schmidt, Ronald, Sr.
2001. Language Policy and Identity Politics in the United States. Philadelphia, PA: Temple University Press.

Schultz, Emily
2002. "Discourse and Politics: Developments in Linguistic Anthropology Since the 1970s." General Anthropology 8(2): 1, 6-7.

Shaul, David L., and N. Louanna Furbee
1998. Language and Culture. Prospect Heights, IL: Waveland Press.

JOURNALS

Ampersand (linguistics newsletter)
　　Elsevier Science, Customer Support Dept.
　　P.O. Box 945
　　New York, NY 10159-0945
　　tel.: 212-633-3730
　　email: usinfo-f@elsevier.com
　　website: http://www.elsevier.nl/homepage/#top

The Internet TESL Journal (available only online)
　　http://www.aitech.ac.jp/~iteslj

Journal of Linguistic Anthropology
　　Society for Linguistic Anthropology
　　c/o Mary Bucholtz, Editor
　　Dept. of Linguistics
　　University of California, Santa Barbara
　　Santa Barbara, CA 93106
　　tel.: 805-893-5415
　　website: http://www.aaanet.org/sla/jla/jlamain.htm

Journal of Sociolinguistics
Blackwell Publishing
350 Main St.
Malden, MA 02148
tel.: 781-388-8200
website: http://www.blackwellpublishers.co.uk/journals/JOSL

Language (published by the Linguistic Society of America)
Archibald Hill, Suite 1325
18th St. NW, #211
Washington, DC 20036-6501
email: language@ling.ohio-state.edu
website: http://www.lsadc.org/language

Language and Communication
Elsevier Science, Ltd.
P.O. Box 945
New York, NY 10159-0945
tel.: 212-633-3730 or 1-888-437-636
email: usinfo-f@elsevier.com
website: http://www.elsevier.com

Language Sciences
Elsevier Science, Ltd.
P.O. Box 945
New York, NY 10159-0945
tel.: 212-633-3730 or 1-888-437-636
email: usinfo-f@elsevier.com
website: http://www.elsevier.com

Linguistics and Education
Elsevier Science, Ltd.
P.O. Box 945
New York, NY 10159-0945
tel.: 212-633-3730 or 1-888-437-636
email: usinfo-f@elsevier.com
website: http://www.elsevier.com

GRADUATE PROGRAMS

Note: Two compilations of university linguistics departments, programs, and centers can be found on the Internet, one at http://www.e.yamagata-u.ac.jp/~t.okada/docs/li_lngst.html and the other at http://www.lsadc.org/webw/programsfr.htm. The graduate programs listed below focus on applied linguistics.

The University of Arizona grants the Ph.D. in anthropology & linguistics through its Department of Linguistics. One programmatic emphasis is on Native American languages & linguistics.
University of Arizona
Department of Linguistics
Tucson, AZ 85721-0028
tel.: 520-621-6897
email: admin@linguistics.arizona.edu
website: w3.arizona.edu/ling

Ball State University incorporates a Program in Applied Linguistics. The M.A. in TESOL and the Ph.D. in English with concentration in applied linguistics are granted through the Department of English.
Ball State University
Department of English
Muncie, IN 47306
tel.: 765-285-8580
email: d000enggrad@bsuvc.bsu.edu
website: http://www.bsu.edu/english/grad/gradgen.html

Brown University offers a Ph.D. program in Cognitive Science and Linguistics through its Department of Cognitive and Linguistic Sciences.
Department of Cognitive and Linguistic Sciences
Brown University
Box 1978
Providence, RI 02912-1978
tel.: 401-863-2616
website: http://www.cog.brown.edu

The University of California, Berkeley offers a Ph.D. program in Social Cultural Anthropology with specializations in a number of domains of application, including linguistic anthropology.
Department of Anthropology
207 Kroeber Hall #3710
Berkeley, CA, 94720
tel.: 510-642-3406
website: http://www.ls.berkeley.edu/dept/anth/phdsoccult.intro

Teachers College, Columbia University, Department of Arts and Humanities, offers a program in Applied Linguistics leading to any of three degrees: the M.A., Ed.M. (Master of Education), or Ed.D. (Doctor of Education).
Teachers College, Columbia University
525 West 120th St., Box 302
New York, NY 10027
tel.: 212-678-3795

website: http://www.teacherscollege.edu/programs/Applied-Linguistics

The University of Hawaii, Manoa, Department of Anthropology, offers a graduate program in leading to the M.A. or Ph.D. degrees with a concentration in "Discursive Practices," which "subsumes, but extends well beyond, the traditional field of linguistic anthropology."
Department of Anthropology
University of Hawaii at Manoa
2424 Maile Way
Honolulu, Hawaii 96822
email: anthprog@hawaii.edu
website: http://www2.soc.hawaii.edu/css/anth/

Indiana University offers graduate degree programs in Anthropology, at both the M.A. and Ph.D. levels, with a specialty in linguistics.
Department of Anthropology
Indiana University
Student Building 130
Bloomington, IN 47405
tel.: 812-855-1041
email: cadamus@indiana.edu
website: http://www.indiana.edu/~anthro

The **State University of New York at Binghamton** grants the Ph.D. in Anthropology with a specialty in linguistic anthropology.
Director of Graduate Studies
Department of Anthropology
Binghamton University
Binghamton, NY 13902-6000
tel.: 607-777-2738
email: pangolin@binghamton.edu

The **State University of New York at Stony Brook** offers a Ph.D. program in Linguistics that includes a focus on "applications in language teaching, speech synthesis and recognition and natural language processing."
Dept. of Linguistics
State University of New York at Stony Brook
SBS Bldg.
Stony Brook, NY 11794-4376
email: sumitchell@notes.cc.sunysb.edu
website: http://semlab2.sbs.sunysb.edu

Oregon State University offers an M.A. program in Applied Anthropology, which provides the opportunity to specialize in one of several areas of applied anthropology including language and cross-cultural communication.

Department of Anthropology
Oregon State University
238 Waldo Hall
Corvallis, OR 97331-6403
tel.: 541-737-4515
email: jyoung@orst.edu

ORGANIZATIONS

Center for Applied Linguistics
4646 40th St., NW
Washington, DC 20016-1859
tel.: 202-362-0700
website: http://www.cal.org/crede

Linguistic Society of America
1325 18th St. NW, Suite 211
Washington, DC 20036-6501
email: lsa@lsadc.org
website: http://www.lsadc.org

Society for Linguistic Anthropology (an AAA section)
American Anthropological Association
American Anthropological Association
1703 New Hampshire Ave., NW
Washington, DC 20009
website: http://www.aaanet.org/sla/index.htm

INFORMATIONAL WEBSITES

Applied Linguistics Virtual Library
http://alt.venus.co.uk/VL/AppLingBBK/VLESL.html

Defense Language Institute
http://www.dli-http://www.army.mil

ERIC Clearinghouse on Urban Education
http://eric-web.tc.columbia.edu

Language and Culture Page
http://www.language-culture.org/

The Linguist List
http://linguistlist.org/

Linguistic Anthropology Sources on the Internet
http://www.brown.edu/Departments/Anthropology/lingsite.html

Linguistic Enterprises: Private Sector Employment for Linguists
http://www.web.gc.cuny.edu/dept/lingu/enter/wylie.htm

Linguistics Career Advice
http://web.gc.cuny.edu/dept/lingu/enter/wylie.htm

National Council for Languages and International Studies
http://www.languagepolicy.org

National Clearinghouse on Bilingual Education
http://www.ncela.gwu.edu

Society for the Study of the Indigenous Languages of the Americas
http://www.ssila.org

Summer Institute of Linguistics (SIL)
http://www.sil.org/

U.S. Office of Bilingual Education
http://www.ed.gov/offices/OBEMLA

PART THREE: NEXT STEPS

20. GAINING ADDITIONAL EXPERIENCE AND EDUCATION IN APPLIED ANTHROPOLOGY

SUGGESTED READINGS

Note: Vol. 19, no. 2 of Practicing Anthropology (Spring, 1997) is a special issue on Masters level practitioners in Anthropology. Vol. 20, no. 4 (Fall, 1998) is a special issue on graduate students applying anthropology.

n.a.
1997, 1998 ed. America's Top Internships (serial publication). New York: Random House

American Anthropological Association
2001. Guide to Departments of Anthropology. Washington, DC: AAA.

Cantrell, Will, and Francine Moderno
1992. International Internships and Volunteer Programs: International Options for Students and Professionals. Oakton, VA : Worldwise.

Council on Social Work Education
1996. Directory of Colleges and Universities with Accredited Social Work Degree Programs. Alexandria, VA: Council on Social Work Education, Inc.

Gliozzo, Charles A., et al. (eds.)
1994. Directory of International Internships -- A World of Opportunities (3rd ed.) East Lansing, MI: Career Development and Placement Services, Michigan State University.

Hyland, Stanley, and Sean Kilpatrick (eds.)
1989. Guide to Training Programs in the Application of Anthropology (3rd ed.) Oklahoma City, OK: SfAA.

Joseph, Rebecca M.
1999. "Making the Most of your Internship." Anthropology Newsletter 40(2) 33.

Kushner, Gilbert

1994. "Training Programs for the Practice of Applied Anthropology." Human Organization 53:186-92.

Kushner, Gilbert, and Alvin Wolfe
1993. "Internship and Practice in Applied Anthropology." Practicing Anthropology 15(1): 3-33.

Nolan, Riall W.
2001. "Teaching Anthropology as if Jobs Mattered." Practicing Anthropology 23(1):58-60.

Omohundro, John
1998. Careers in Anthropology. MountainView, CA: Mayfield Press.

Owens, Walter
1993. "Competing in the Market Place." Practicing Anthropology 15(1):22-24.

Price, Laurie J.
2001. "The Mismatch Between Anthropology Graduate Training and the Work Lives of Graduates." Practicing Anthropology 23(1):55-60.

Schlotter, Jeffrey
1993. "The Internship as a Vehicle to Identity." Practicing Anthropology 15(1):16-18.

Simonelli, Jeanne
2001. "Mainstreaming the Applied Track: Connections, Guises, and Concerns." Practicing Anthropology 23(1):48-49.

Singer, Merrill (ed.), et al.
1994. Anthropologists at Work: Responses to Student Questions About Anthropology Careers. Washington, DC: NAPA.

Squires Susan
2000. "What Your Advisor Will Never Tell You." In Sabloff, Paula L.W. (ed.): Careers in Anthropology: Profiles of Practitioner Anthropologists (NAPA Bulletin no. 20), pp., 67-70. Washington, DC: American Anthropological Association.

INFORMATIONAL WEBSITES

AFOB (Archaeological Fieldwork Opportunities Bulletin) Online http:www.archaeological.org/webinfo.php?page=10015

AMSA (American Medical Student Association) Resources (site contains lists of summer programs and internships)
http://www.amsa.org

Archaeological Fieldwork Opportunities (list of excavations seeking volunteers)
http://www.cincpac.com/afos/testpit.html

Association of Schools of Public Health (site includes a page of internships and fellowships)
http://www.asph.org

D'Gap Internships
http://www.developmentgapl.org/intern.html

Federal Student Work Experience Program (FSWEP)
http://www.jobs.gc.ca/fswep-pfete/student/index_e.htm

Getting a Summer Job in Archaeology
http://www.anthro.umt.edu/jobs/sumjobar.htm

Graduate Programs in Applied Anthropology
http://www.anthap.oakland.edu/gradprog.htm

Graduate Programs in Bioethics
http://www.ajobonline.com/gra_program.php
http://www.gradschools.com/listings/menus/ethics_menu.html

Graduate Programs in Environmental Ethics
http://www.cep.unt.edu/other.html for a list of

Graduate Programs in Criminology, Criminal Justice, and Related Fields
http://www.unl.edu/eskridge/GRADLINKS.html

GradSchools.com
http://www.gradscdhools.com/search.html

Guidelines for Training Practicing Anthropologists – 1995
http://www.anthap.oakland.edu/guidelin.htm

Internship Programs
http://www.internshipprograms.com

Jobtrak Summer Jobs and Internships

http://www.jobtrak.com

Jobs and Internships in Anthropology
http://www.online.sfsu.edu/~mgriffin/jobs.html

University of Massachusetts Medical School, International Health Care
Opportunities Clearinghouse
http://www.library.ummed.edu/ihoc

MBA (Masters of Business Administration) Programs (some with a
business anthropology or social marketing concentration)
http://www.bus.ualberta.ca/informs.

Museum Training Opportunities for Anthropology Students
http://www.nmnh.si.edu/cma/surveyhtml

Overseas Development Student Network
http://www.igc.apc.org/odn

SRA (Society of Research Administrators International) Grants Web
http://www.srainternational.org/newweb/

21. FINDING A JOB AS AN APPLIED ANTHROPOLOGIST

SUGGESTED READINGS

Bennett, Linda A. (ed.)
1988. Bridges for Changing Times: Local Practitioner Organizations in American Anthropology (NAPA Bulletin No. 6). Washington, DC: National Association for the Practice of Anthropology.

Bolles, Richard Nelson
2001. What Color is Your Parachute? A Practical Manual for job Hunters and Career Changers. Berkeley, CA: Ten Speed Press.

Burcaw, G. Ellis
1997. Introduction to Museum Work. Walnut Creek, CA: AltaMira Press.

Camenson, Blythe
1998. Opportunities in Zoos and Aquariums. Lincolnwood, IL: VGM Career Horizons.

2000. Great Jobs for Anthropology Majors. Lincolnwood, IL: VGM Publishing.

Camino, Linda A.
2000. "Working as an Independent Consultant." In Sabloff, Paula L.W. (ed.): Careers in Anthropology: Profiles of Practitioner Anthropologists (NAPA Bulletin no. 20), pp. 45-48. Washington, DC: American Anthropological Association.

Clarke, Mari H.
2000. "On the Road Again: International Development Consulting." In Sabloff, Paula L.W. (ed.): Careers in Anthropology: Profiles of Practitioner Anthropologists (NAPA Bulletin no. 20), pp. 71-74. Washington, DC: American Anthropological Association.

Doelling, Carol N.
1997. Social Work Career Development: a Handbook for Job Hunting and Career Planning. Washington, DC: National Association of Social Workers.

Emener, W., and M. Darrow (eds.)

1991. <u>Career Explorations in Human Services</u>. Springfield, IL: Charles C. Thomas.

Ferrante, Joan
1997. <u>Let's Go Anthropology: Travels on the Internet</u>. Belmont, CA: Wadsworth.

Fowler, Don D., and Donald L. Hardesty (eds.)
1994. <u>Others Knowing Others: Perspectives on Ethnographic Careers</u>. Washington, DC: Smithsonian Institution Press.

Garner, Geraldine O.
1993. <u>Careers in Social and Rehabilitation Services</u>. Lincolnwood, IL: VGM Career Horizons

Ginsberg, Leon H.
1998. <u>Careers in Social Work</u>. Boston: Allyn and Bacon.

Hanson, Karen J. (ed.)
1988. <u>Mainstreaming Anthropology: Experiences in Government Employment</u> (NAPA Bulletin No. 5). Washington, DC: National Association for the Practice of Anthropology.

Jordan, Ann T.
1994 (ed.). <u>Practicing Anthropology in Corporate America: Consulting on Organizational Culture</u> (NAPA Bulletin No. 14). Washington, DC: National Association for the Practice of Anthropology.

Kay, Andrea G.
1996. <u>Interview Strategies That Will Get You the Job You Want.</u> Whitehall, VA: Betterway Publications.

1997. <u>Resumes That Will Get You the Job You Want</u>. Whitehall, VA: Betterway Publications.

Kuehnast, Kathleen
1999. "Career Options Outside the Academy." <u>Anthropology Newsletter</u> 40(2):32.

Luce, Randall C.
1990. "Anthropologists and Private, Humanitarian Aid Agencies." In Chaiken, Miriam S., and Anne K. Fleuret (eds.): <u>Social Change and Applied Anthropology: Essays in Honor of David W. Brokensha</u>, pp. 32-42. Boulder, CO: Westview Press.

Manderson, Lenore (ed.)
1996. "Handbook and Manuals in Applied Research." Practicing Anthropology 18(3):3-40 (special issue).

Nemeth, Charles P.
1991. Anderson's Directory of Criminal Justice Education, 1991. Cincinnati, OH: Anderson Publ. Co.

Omohundro, John T.
2000. Careers in Anthropology (2nd ed.). New York: McGraw-Hill.

Quirk, Kathleen, and Marsha Jenakovich
1997. "Anthropologists Practicing with Masters' Degrees: Introduction." Practicing Anthropology 19(2)2-6.

Sabloff, Paula L.W. (ed.)
2000. Careers in Anthropology: Profiles of Practitioner Anthropologists (NAPA Bulletin no. 20). Washington, DC: American Anthropological Association.

Skreija, Andris
1998. "Tips for Job Hunters: The Vita and Cover Letter." Anthropology Newsletter 39(7):29.

Stapp, Darby
2000. "Putting Anthropology to Work." In Sabloff, Paula L.W. (ed.): Careers in Anthropology: Profiles of Practitioner Anthropologists (NAPA Bulletin no. 20), pp. 5-7. Washington, DC: American Anthropological Association.

Stephens, W. Richard
2003. Careers in Anthropology: What an Anthropology Degree Can Do For You. Boston: Allyn and Bacon.

Stinchcomb, James D.
1990. Opportunities in Law Enforcement and Criminal Justice Careers. Lincolnwood, IL: VGM Career Horizons.

Stone, John V.
1993. "Professional Networks." Practicing Anthropology 15(1):25-27.

Tice, Karin E.
2000. "Engaging Anthropology in the Nonprofit Sector." In Sabloff, Paula L.W. (ed.): Careers in Anthropology: Profiles of Practitioner Anthropologists, pp. 31-33. Washington, DC: National Association for the Practice of Anthropology.

Trainor, Theresa
1997. "Formulating a Practitioner Identity." Practicing Anthropology
19(2):7-10.

van Willigen, John
1991. Anthropology in Use: A Sourcebook on Anthropological
Practice. Boulder, CO: Westview Press.

Wilson, Ruth P.
1998. "The Role of Anthropologists as Short-Term Consultants."
Human Organization 57(2):245-252.

Wittenberg, Renee
1996. Opportunities in Social Work Careers. Lincolnwood, IL:
VGM Career Horizons.

ORGANIZATIONS FACILITATING JOB SEARCHES

Note: Below is a list of some of the many that provide job postings in publications or on the Web, or conduct periodic job fairs.

American Anthropological Association (conducts placement interviews at annual meeting; hosts AAA Career Center on the Internet at the website below; publishes Job Placement Column in Anthropology News)
    4350 North Fairfax Drive, Suite 640
    Arlington, VA 22203-1620
    tel.: 703-528-1902
    fax: 703/528-3546
    website: http://www.aaa.net (annual meeting info.) or
    http://www.aaanet.org/careers/htm

American Association of Physical Anthropologists (publishes a pamphlet on careers in physical anthropology; request at email address below)
    P.O. Box 1897
    Lawrence, KS 66044-8897
    email: cwienker@cfrvm.usf.edu
    website: http://www.physanth.org

Global Health Council (conducts job fair at annual meeting)
    The Global Health Council
    1701 K Street, NW
    Washington, DC, 20006
    tel.: 202-833-5900
    email: ghc@globalhealth.org

website: http://www.globalhealth.org

National Association of Student Anthropologists
  American Anthropological Association
  4350 North Fairfax Drive, Suite 640
  Arlington, VA 22203-1620
  tel.: 703-528-1902
  website: http://www.aaanet.org.nasa

National Association for the Practice of Anthropology (numerous job-related publications)
  American Anthropological Association
  4350 North Fairfax Drive, Suite 640
  Arlington, VA 22203-1620
  tel.: 703-528-1902
  website: http://www.aaanet.org/napa

National Association of Colleges and Employers
  62 Highland Ave.
  Bethlehem, PA 18017-9085
  tel.: 610-868-1421 or 1-800-544-5272
  website: http://jobweb

Society for American Archaeology (posts job announcements at web address below)
  900 Second St., NE, #12
  Washington, DC 20002-3557
  tel.: 202-789-8200
  email: headquarters@saa.org
  website: http://www.saa.org/Careers/job-listing.html

Society for Applied Anthropology (publishes job opportunities online at web address below)
  P.O. Box 2436
  Oklahoma City, OK 73101-2436
  tel.: 405-843-8553
  email: info@sfaa.net
  website: http://www.sfaa.net, click on "employment"

Society for Historical Archaeology (publishes "Careers in Historical Archaeology"; maintains website of same name at web address below)
  PO Box 30446
  Tucson, AZ 85751-0446
  tel.: 520-886-8006
  website: http:// www.sha.org/sha_cbro.htm

INFORMATIONAL WEBSITES

Note: see also websites, listed in individual domain chapters above, of multilateral and bilateral organizations such as the World Health Organization, USAID, etc., which hire applied anthropologists.

American Anthropological Association On-line Career Center
http://www.aaanet.jobcontrolcenter.com

American Medical Student Association Online (lists international health opportunities)
http://www.amsa.org/tf/inthlth

America's Job Bank
http://www.ajb.dni.us

Anthropologists at Work: Responses to Student Questions About Anthropology Careers
http://www.anthap.oakland.edu/napafaq.htm

Anthropologists in the Corporate Setting
http://www.nku.edu/~anthro/anthrocareers.jpg

AnthroTECH Career Connection (online company that publishes classified ads for jobs, internships or volunteer opportunities in anthropology)
http://www.anthrotech.com/career/

Archaeologyfieldwork.com (archaeology employment listings and volunteer opportunities)
http://www.archaeologyfieldwork.com/

Association of Schools of Public Health: Internships and Fellowships
http://www.asph.org/intfel.htm

Aviso Employment Resources Online (job bank for museum professionals)
http://aviso.aam-us.org

CareerBuilder.com
http://www.careerbuilder.com/JobSeeker

Careers at the UN
http://www.icsc.un.org/vab/index.htm

Careers in Anthropology
http://www.aaanet.org/careersbroch.htm

Careers in Anthropology: Where the Jobs Are
http://www.nku.edu/~anthro/careers.html#careers

Careers in Historical Archaeology
http://www.sha.org/sha_cbro.htm

Careers in Physical Anthropology
http://www.physanth.org/careers

Catapult Summer Jobs and Internships
http://www.jobweb.org/catapult/jintern.htm

Chronicle of Higher Education Career Network
http://www.jobs.chronicle.com/jobs/10/300/1500

Context-Based Research Group
http://www.anthrojobl.com/

Environment and Society Internet Resource Guide
http://www.rpi.edu/dept/environ/guide

Ethics Jobs Online
http://www.ethicsjobs.ca

Federal Government Jobs
http:www.usajobs.opm.gov

Finding a Job in Anthropology
http://www.anthro.umt.edu/jobs

Forensic Anthropology: Frequently Asked Questions
http://people.uncw.edu/albertm/faqs.htm

Forensic Science Jobs
http://www.aafs.org/employ/list1.htm

Getting a Job in Archaeology
http://www.anthro.umt.edu/jobs/sumjobar.htm

Getting Past Go
http://www.mongen.com/getgo

The Global Health Network (contains information on jobs in global health)
http://www.pitt.edu/HOME/GHNet/GHNet.html

Govtjobs.com (state and local government job opportunities)
http://www.govtjobs.com

Health Promotion Career Network
http://www.hpcareer.net

H-Net Job Guide for the Humanities and Social Sciences
http://www.matrix.msu.edu/jobs/

Idealist.org (lists over 28,000 nonprofit and community organizations
worldwide; contains job, internship, and volunteer opportunities)
http://www.idealist.org

International Career Employment Weekly
http://www.internationaljobs.org

International Health Care Opportunities Clearinghouse
http://www.library.ummed.edu/ihoc

Jobs and Internships in Anthropology
http://www.online.sfsu.edu/~mgriffin/jobs.html

Jobs in Health and Sciences Resource List
http://www.tulane.edu/~dmsander/garryfavwebjobs.html

Jobweb
http://www.jobwweb.com

Linguistic Enterprises: Private Sector Employment for Linguists
http://www.web.gc.cuny.edu/dept/lingu/enter/wylie.htm

Medical Anthropology Positions Open and Positions Wanted
http://www.medanth.com/positions

Monster.com
http://www.jobsearch.monster.com/jobsearch.asp?cy=US&q=
anthropology

NASWJobLink (The Social Work Employment Line)
http://www.naswdc.org/JOB.HTM

NGOs, PVOs and Foundations (list of major NGOs, PVOs, and private charitable foundations, many of which employ applied anthropologists)
http://www.foundationcenter.org

Non-Academic Careers in Physical Anthropology
http://www.weber.ucsd.edu/~jmoore/bioanthro/brochure2.html

Non-profit Jobs and Career Opportunities
http://www.opportunitynocs.org

Opportunity Knocks (Jobs in non-profit organizations)
http://www.opportunitynocs.org

Peace Corps
http://www.peacecorps.gov/home.html

Postdoctoral Opportunities in Anthropology
http://www.unm.edu/~acstone/postdocs/post-doc.html

Primate-Jobs
http://www.primate.wisc.edu/pin/jobs/index.html

Resume Building
http://www.nku.edu/~acs/resume.html

Shovelbums (jobs in archaeology)
http://www.anthro.umt.edu/jobs/shovelbums.htm

So You Want to Be a Forensic Anthropologist?
http://www.anthro.umt.edu/studguide/forensic.htm

Social Marketing Job Bank
http://www.social-marketing.com/jobbank

Social Work and Social Services Jobs Online
http://www.gwbweb.wustl.edu/jobs/links.html

Social Work Careers
http://www.socialworkrs.org/profession/default.asp

Social Work Job Openings
http://www.socialservice.com

Society for American Archaeology Job Announcements
http://www.saa.org/careers/job-listing.html

Smithsonian Jobs
http://www.anthro.umt.edu/jobs/smithsonian.htm

StudentJobs (government employment opportunities for students)
http://www.studentjobs.gov/

UN Jobs Newsletter
http://www.cuenet.com/archive/globalj/97-01/msg0008.html

University of Massachusetts Medical School International Health Care
Opportunities Clearinghouse
http://www.library.ummed.edu/ihoc

USAJobs (government employment opportunities)
http://www.usajobs.opm.gov/

U.S. Museum Jobs Online
http://www.museum-employment.com

LOCAL PRACTITIONER ORGANIZATIONS

Chicago Association for Practicing Anthropologists
Roger P. McConochie
President. Global Vision Inst.
2400 E. Main St., Suite 103-A
St. Charles, IL 60174-2414
tel.: 630-584-5700
email.: 73500.1170@compuserve.com

Great Lakes Association of Practicing Anthropologists
Linda Easley
5750 Prospect Hill Road
Gross Lake, MI 49240
tel.: 313-428-7514
email: lindaeasle@aol.com

High Plains Society for Applied Anthropology (HPSfAA)
Lenora Bohren
3621 South Taft
Loveland CO 80537
tel.: 970-669-6192
email: bohren@cahs.colostate.edu

Mid-South Association of Practicing Anthropologists

Cindy Martin
Dept. of Anthropology
University of Memphis
Memphis, TN 38152
tel.: 901-678-2080
email: cmartin@msuvx2.memphis.edu

North Florida Network of Practicing Anthropologists
Roberta Hammond
125 Cadiz St.
Tallahassee, FL 32301
tel.: 904-222-7945
email: rmhammond@worldnet.att.net

Philadelphia Association of Practicing Anthropologists
Elaine Simon
Urban Studies Program
University of Pennsylvania
130 McNeil Bldg.
Philadelphia, PA 19104-6209
tel.:215-898-1182
email: esimon@mail.sas.upenn.edu

Southern California Applied Anthropology Network
Stephen C. Maack
2872 Nicada Drive
Los Angeles, CA 90077-2024
tel.: 310-475-7962
email: scmaack@delphi.com

Sun Coast Organization of Practicing Anthropologists
Alayne Unterberger
Moffitt Cancer Center and Research Institute
12902 Magnolia Drive
Tampa, FL 33612
tel.: 813-632-1344
email: alayne@moffitt.usf.edu

Washington Association of Professional Anthropologists
Bill Roberts
Dept. of Anthropology and Sociology
St. Mary's College of Maryland
St. Mary's City, MD 20686
tel.: 301-862-0387
julieroberts@worldnet.att.net

WEBSITES OF U.S. GOVERNMENT OFFICES

Agency for International Development (USAID)
http://www.info.usaid.gov

Bureau of Indian Affairs (BIA)
http://www.doi.gov/bureau-indian-affairs.html

Department of Defense
http://www.defenselink.mil/

Department of Veterans Affairs
http://www.va.gov/

Department of Health and Human Services
http://www.dhhs.gov/

Department of Housing and Urban Development
http://www.hud.gov/

Federal Emergency Management Agency
http://www.fema.gov/

Immigration and Naturalization Service
http://www.ins.usdoj.gov/

Indian Health Service
http://www.ihs.gov

National Institutes of Health
http://www.nih.gov/

National Park Service
http://www.nps.gov/

Peace Corps
http://www.peacecorps.gov

Smithsonian Institution
http://www.si.edu

Social Security Administration
http://www.ssa.gov/

NOTES

NOTES

NOTES

NOTES

NOTES

NOTES